T0347132

Merchants
and
Colonialism

Other Titles in the Series

Social Science across Disciplines is a
new series that brings to a general audience
a selection from the papers and lectures
delivered at the Centre for Studies in
Social Sciences, Calcutta (CSSSC), over
the last four decades. They fall into two
categories—first, a selection from among
the Occasional Papers circulated by the
Centre's faculty, and second, from the two
series of memorial lectures in the name of
Sakharam Ganesh Deuskar (for lectures on
Indian History and Culture) and of Romesh
Chunder Dutt (for lectures on Political
Economy).

Amiya Kumar Bagchi

Merchants and Colonialism

Introduction by
Lakshmi Subramanian

Centre for Studies
in Social Sciences, Calcutta

OXFORD
UNIVERSITY PRESS

OXFORD
UNIVERSITY PRESS

Oxford University Press is a department of the University of Oxford.
It furthers the University's objective of excellence in research, scholarship,
and education by publishing worldwide. Oxford is a registered trademark of
Oxford University Press in the UK and in certain other countries.

Published in India by
Oxford University Press
2/11 Ground Floor, Ansari Road, Daryaganj, New Delhi 110 002, India

ISBN-13 (print edition): 978-0-19-948668-7
ISBN-10 (print edition): 0-19-948668-9

ISBN-13 (eBook): 978-0-19-909564-3
ISBN-10 (eBook): 0-19-909564-7

Typeset in Berling LT Std 10/14
by Tranistics Data Technologies, Kolkata 700 091
Printed in India by Replika Press Pvt. Ltd

Contents

About the Author

Amiya Kumar Bagchi is a distinguished Political Economist who has contributed to the Marxist perspective, development studies, and political economy. He graduated in Economics from Presidency College, Calcutta, and received his PhD from the University of Cambridge, UK. A former Professor at the Centre for Studies in Social Sciences, Calcutta (CSSSC) (1974–2001), he was its Director from 1988 to 1997. He has taught at the University of Cambridge, École des hautes études en sciences sociales, Paris, and Cornell University, USA, among other places. Bagchi was also the Founder-Director of the Institute of Development Studies, Kolkata, India. Among his many books are *Private Investment in India* (1972), *The Political Economy of Development* (1982), *The Evolution of the State Bank of India*, in 2 volumes (1987, 1989), *Capital and Labour Redefined: India and the Third World* (2002), *The Developmental State* *in History and in the Twentieth Century* (2004), and *Colonialism and the Indian Economy* (2010). He has also written extensively in Bengali. Bagchi received the VKRV Rao Award for Economics in 1980.

About the Editors

Partha Chatterjee is Professor of Anthropology and of Middle Eastern, South Asian and African Studies at Columbia University, New York, USA. A member of the CSSSC faculty for 36 years, he was also its Director from 1997 to 2007, and continues as Honorary Professor of Political Science. Among his books are *Nationalist Thought and the Colonial World* (1986), *The Nation and Its Fragments: Colonial and Postcolonial Histories* (1993), *A Princely Impostor? The Strange and Universal History of the Kumar of Bhawal* (2001), *The Politics of the Governed* (2004), and *The Black Hole of Empire* (2012).

Rosinka Chaudhuri is Director and Professor of Cultural Studies at the CSSSC. She is also the first Mellon Professor of the Global South at the University of Oxford. She has written *Gentlemen Poets in Colonial Bengal* (2002), *Freedom and Beef Steaks* (2012), and

The Literary Thing (2013) and edited *Derozio, Poet of India* (2008), *The Indian Postcolonial* (co-edited, 2010), *A History of Indian Poetry in English* (2016), and *An Acre of Green Grass and Other English Writings of Buddhadeva Bose* (2018). She has also translated and introduced *Rabindranath Tagore: Letters from a Young Poet* (2014).

About the Introduction Writer

Lakshmi Subramanian taught at Visva-Bharati, Santiniketan, and Jamia Millia Islamia, New Delhi, and was Professor of History at the CSSSC from 2002 to 2007 and from 2010 to 2018. She is currently an Associate Fellow at the Nantes Institute for Advanced Study, France, and Scholar in Residence at Godrej Archives, Mumbai. Her research interests include Social and Economic history of India and the Indian Ocean as well as the history of music and performance practices in south India. She has several publications to her credit including *Three Merchants of Bombay* (2012) and *Indigenous Capital and Imperial Expansion: Bombay, Surat and the West Coast* (1996). Her most recent work is titled *The Sovereign and the Pirate: Ordering Maritime Subjects in India's Western Littoral* (2016).

General Introduction to the Series

Partha Chatterjee and *Rosinka Chaudhuri*

This series of publications from Oxford University Press brings to a general audience a selection of the papers and lectures delivered at the Centre for Studies in Social Sciences, Calcutta (CSSSC), over the last four decades. They fall into two categories: first, a chosen few from among the Occasional Papers circulated by the Centre's faculty and second, from the two series of memorial lectures in the name of Sakharam Ganesh Deuskar, for lectures on Indian history and culture, and Romesh Chunder Dutt, for lectures on political economy.

The CSSSC was founded in 1973 as an autonomous research institute financed primarily by the Indian Council for Social Science Research and the Government of West Bengal. Since then, the Centre, as it is ubiquitously known, has established an academic reputation that places it at the crest of research institutes of excellence in India. Its faculty works in the fields of history, political science, sociology, social anthropology, geography, economics, and cultural studies. Its unique interdisciplinary culture allows for collaborations between scholars from different fields of research that might not find support in traditional department-based institutions, attracting students and researchers from across the country and abroad.

The R.C. Dutt Lectures at the CSSSC have focused on themes from economic theory, economic history, and development policy, mostly relating to India. As is well known, Romesh Chunder Dutt (1848–1909) served in the Indian Civil Service from 1871 to 1897. On retirement, he lectured at the University of London, UK, and wrote his classic work in two volumes, *The Economic History of India under Early British Rule* (1902) and *The Economic History of India in the Victorian Age* (1904). He was elected president of the 1899 session of the Indian National Congress. Apart from his extensive writings on the colonial economy, the condition of the peasantry, famines, and land rights, Dutt was also a poet in English and a novelist in Bengali, writing on historical and social themes. Over the years, some of the most eminent economists of India have delivered the R.C. Dutt lectures at the Centre. Among them are Sukhamoy Chakrabarti, K.N. Raj, V.M. Dandekar, Ashok Rudra, Krishna Bharadwaj, A. Vaidyanathan, Suresh Tendulkar, Prabhat Patnaik, I.S. Gulati, Amit Bhaduri, C.T. Kurien, Praveen Visaria, Kaushik Basu, Geeta Sen, Debraj Ray, Abhijit V. Banerjee, Ravi Kanbur, and Dilip Mookerjee. The lectures selected for publication in the present series will capture key debates among Indian economists in the last four decades in topics such as the crisis of planning, economic liberalization, inequality, gender and development, sustainable growth, and the effects of globalization.

The S.G. Deuskar Lectures began as a series on Indian nationalism but widened to reflect the cross-disciplinary interests the CSSSC nurtured, featuring a range of distinguished speakers on the history, culture, politics, and society of India. Sakharam Ganesh Deuskar (1869–1912) was Maharashtrian by ancestry and member of a family that migrated in the mid-eighteenth century to the Santal Parganas on the border of Bihar and Bengal. A schoolteacher and journalist by profession, he is best known for his Bengali tract *Desher Katha* (1904)—a damning indictment of the exploitative and violent character of British colonial rule—which is reported to have sold 13,000 copies in five editions within five years during the Swadeshi movement in Bengal. Some of the finest scholars and artists of modern India have delivered the Deuskar Lectures, including, among historians, Ranajit Guha, Tapan Raychaudhuri, Irfan Habib, Satish Chandra, Romila Thapar, Partha Sarathi Gupta, Sabyasachi Bhattacharya, Sumit Sarkar, Dipesh Chakrabarty, Muzaffar Alam, Gyanendra Pandey, Sanjay Subrahmanyam, and Shahid Amin; among philosophers, J.N. Mohanty and Bimal Krishna Matilal; among artists and art critics, Geeta Kapur, Vivan Sundaram, K.G. Subramanyan, and Ghulam Mohammed Sheikh; among social theorists, Gayatri Chakravorty Spivak, Sudipta Kaviraj, and Veena Das. A selection of these lectures will now be reprinted in this current initiative from Oxford University Press.

Occasional Papers published by the CSSSC represent the research of the CSSSC faculty over the years. Many of these papers were later published in journals and books, some becoming classic essays that are essential reading for students and researchers in the field. Some of the most important works in the Indian social sciences, it would be fair to say, are represented here in the form of papers or drafts of book chapters. Of the nearly 200 Occasional Papers published so far, we will reprint in the present series only those that are not already in wide circulation as journal articles or book chapters. Included among our Occasional Papers will be the current initiative of the Archives Series Occasional Papers, meant specifically to showcase the collection in the CSSSC visual archives.

By turning these outstanding papers into little books that stand on their own, our series is not intended as a survey of disciplinary fields. Rather, the intention is to present to the reader within a concise format an intellectual encounter with some of the foremost practitioners in the field of humanities and social sciences in India. R.K. Narayan, in his childhood memoir, *My Days* (1947), had written that when, as young men, he and his friends had discussed starting a journal and were thinking of names for it, someone suggested 'Indian Thought'. 'There is no such thing' was the witty response from a friend. Narayan nevertheless began publishing *Indian Thought*, a quarterly of literature, philosophy, and culture, which lasted all of one year. We suggest that this series might, in the end, prove his friend wrong.

Introduction

Lakshmi Subramanian

The workings and ramifications of colonial power and their impact in distorting capitalist development in India have been key and recurrent concerns in the work of Amiya Kumar Bagchi. In many ways, as we shall see, his Occasional Paper (OP) 'Merchants and Colonialism'[1] was a trendsetter, an early and prescient indication of not only his subsequent expositions on colonialism but also of a number of trends in historical research that became influential in the decade of the 1980s. Responding to some of the scholarship that had emerged then, especially in the subfield of maritime history, the paper retains the author's theoretical convictions on the structural damage and distortions that colonialism produced. It adopts, on the whole, a Marxist framework in relation to the transition to capitalism debate, which has remained at the heart of Indian economic history notwithstanding significant mutations and shifts in emphases.

This introduction is, therefore, an exercise in locating the OP within the larger and older milieu of historiography as a means to flag some of its central formulations and in reviewing more recent work in the field that may help us grapple with the significance of colonialism as a framing device in a longue durée history of Indian merchant behaviour. The 1980s saw a more nuanced revision of the older debates on the eighteenth century, viewed largely as a period of decline leading to the British colonial regime, which in its workings was destructive of existing social relations of production. As early as 1971, Philip Calkins had alerted us to the regionalization of Mughal authority in the first half of the eighteenth century and to the new centrality that merchants and scribal groups assumed in regional apparatuses of power.[2] Not that merchants had not been important in the Mughal state, but simply that their functions significantly expanded in course of the century of decline, making them potential agents of larger societal transformation. Bagchi begins his paper by looking at the power and potential that merchants had in both pre-capitalist as well as in not fully capitalist societies; he follows it with the sociology of merchant responses to British colonial paramountcy and reflects on the origins of industrial capitalism in India. Arguing from the vantage point of Marxist assumptions about transition of merchant capital and artisanal energy to industrial capital, the paper makes a strong case for the impact of colonialism on merchant and manufacturing society, and on the changes in the internal organization of merchants who had to opt for survival strategies. A superficial reading may give the impression that Bagchi— whose paper appeared two years prior to C.A. Bayly's book *Rulers, Townsmen and Bazaars*—is being apologetic about merchant behaviour and responses in contrast to the ways in which Bayly would foreground merchants and bazaars in his analysis of Indian society on the eve of and during the early stages of colonial expansion.[3] However, what Bagchi in fact does is identify the striations in merchant society, the mode of their interactions with artisans, and the pressures that colonial expansion and rule put on merchant and manufacturing society, which precluded any likelihood of a transition to capitalist society. For Bagchi, the merchant-collaborator was not the protagonist and unqualified beneficiary of colonial expansion;

rather, he was a strategist looking out for any avenues for survival.

One striking feature of the paper is its integration of some of the most significant formulations to come from the work in the 1970s and early 1980s on India's maritime history. By this time, thanks to the work of Dasgupta, Pearson, and others, the significance of Asian trade and the scale of operations of Asian merchants who functioned in a complex setting of empires and markets were evident.[4] Bagchi is careful to record these advances in scholarship even while reiterating his critique of colonial mechanisms that subverted existing arrangements of free and fair trade in the high seas and of European intention to capture the major part of the gains from intra-Asian and Indo-European trade (p. 15). In fact, Bagchi's view is not entirely tenable since we know that the volume of trade in the Indian Ocean that was largely dominated by Indian merchants was significantly more than that of the trade between India and Europe, and that it was only after the simultaneous decline of the empires of Persia, India, and Turkey that markets in the Indian Ocean failed to sustain traffic. So, even if British designs to exercise monopoly and monopsony control were in full display from the beginning of the eighteenth century, it does not appear to have had sufficient impact before the actual political revolutions that were affected in and after 1757.

On the other hand, the paper makes a strong and persuasive argument pointing out the long-term de-industrialization that accompanied colonial rule and which had the perverse effect of decimating the ranks of those independent artisans who had close links with the merchants and of those merchants who had close links with craft industries. Reading the documentation of the East India Company, Bagchi refers to the crises that affected cotton and silk production and manufacture in Bengal and to the irreversible consequences they produced. The essentials of his argument have remained important to the debate on de-industrialization: that the East India Company was instrumental in producing structural changes in the organization of textile production, especially in Bengal, and that weavers suffered as a consequence are now common sense. So even if there are exponents of the demand and supply argument, namely, that Bengal textiles were no longer in demand in the European economy from the nineteenth century, it is now beyond doubt that the production process was subject to severe pressure and that the weaver was transformed from a price worker to a wage worker whose legal status was subject to serious modification. The real challenge, in fact, is to square up social experience with economic change; subsequent research on the responses of merchants and manufacturers did attempt to do this and the impression that emerges strongly is of a beleaguered weaving community grappling with a structural crisis that was as much to do with the shock to the economy as with the structural changes that the Company brought in.[5] Some fared better than others, especially merchants, but the facts to be remembered are the fragility of their operations and their falling back on strategies that remained familial and community-centred. Here there were regional variations and Bagchi was among the first to identify the contrast between Bengal and Bombay.

The establishment of formal colonial rule and the articulation of the colonial trading economy by the end of the eighteenth and the beginning of the nineteenth century marked a new phase in the subordination of India. There, too, regional variations existed as far as the impact of colonial rule was concerned; the paper correctly identifies the consequences of the delayed colonial conquest in western India to explain Bombay's resilience in contrast to Bengal's subjugation. We now know how important this argument has been in understanding the nature of capital and commercial development in Bombay and western India and how this has provided a useful basis for later research into Parsi and Gujarati capital formation in nineteenth-century western India. Amar Farooqui, Asiya Siddiqi, and Claude Markovits, among many others, built on this formulation to analyse Bombay's commercial society, which was able to withstand several global and trade shocks and retain its interest and investment in capital accumulation and industrial start-ups.[6]

As mentioned earlier, the paper has a prescient quality to it in the sense that it has been able to track most of the major themes and sub-fields that have come to characterise recent economic history and sociology. This is especially true in the section related to law and legal cultures constitutive of differential economic behaviour and success. Bagchi refers to the paradoxical circumstances in which communities under the more progressive system of law were wiped out while those who survived happened to be under some variant of the less progressive system of Mitākshara law. Why this paradoxical event occurred and functioned is not easy to determine; in fact, not much work has been done on law and merchant behaviour. Bagchi suggests that jointly held mercantile properties were less vulnerable to the demands of creditors, and was, in its broad essentials, more appropriate for the continuation of the familial nature of Indian businesses.

The workings of Indian businesses and trade have remained a subject of historical interest and investigation. What was it that enabled Indian traders and bankers to run operations in conditions of political change and economic dislocation, especially during the eighteenth and nineteenth centuries? Was it their relatively lower operational costs that helped them tide over crises? Was it a specialized system of trust and reciprocity that was associated with specific communities and family networks? Or was it a combination of pragmatic business practice and acumen that enabled merchants to respond to global demand and change and even subvert the authority of the colonial state? Recent sociological literature would point in such a direction without discounting the severity of colonial impact. It is here that Bagchi's paper serves as a useful reminder to take a closer look at the distortions that colonial articulations produced which precluded an easy transition to the level of economic activity and organization that we have come to see as sustainable in terms of capitalist progression.

Notes and References

1. Occasional Paper 38, 'Merchants and Colonialism', Centre for Studies in Social Sciences, Calcutta, September 1981.
2. Philip B. Calkins, 'The Formation of a Regionally Oriented Ruling Group in Bengal', *Journal of Asian Studies* XXIX (1970).
3. C.A. Bayly, *Rulers, Townsmen and Bazaars: North Indian Society in the Age of Imperial Expansion 1770–1870* (Cambridge: Cambridge University Press, 1983).
4. M.N. Pearson, *Merchants and Rulers in Gujarat: The Response to the Portuguese in the Sixteenth Century* (Berkeley: University of California Press, 1976); Ashin Dasgupta, *Indian Merchants and the Decline of Surat circa 1700–1750* (Wiesbaden: Franz Verlag, 1979).
5. Hameeda Hossain, *The Company Weavers of Bengal: The East India Company and the*

Organization of Textile Production in Bengal, 1750–1813 (New Delhi: Oxford University Press, 1986); D.B. Mitra, *Cotton Weavers of Bengal* (Calcutta: Firma K.L.M., 1978).

6. Asiya Siddiqi, ed., *Trade and Finance in Colonial India 1750–1860* (New Delhi: Oxford University Press, 1995); see also Asiya Siddiqi, 'The Business World of Jamsetjee Jejeebhoy', *Indian Economic and Social History Review* XIX, nos 3–4 (1982): 302–24; Amar Farooqui, *Opium City: The Making of Early Victorian Bombay* (New Delhi: Three Essays, 2006); Claude Markovits, 'Bombay as a Business Centre in the Colonial Period', in *Merchants, Traders, Entrepreneurs: Indian Business in the Colonial Era* edited by Claude Markovits (Basingstoke: Palgrave Macmillan, 2008).

Merchants
and
Colonialism

AMIYA KUMAR BAGCHI

Merchant Capital and Pre-capitalist Social Formations

Merchants form a component of a capitalist class in a developed capitalist economy (that is, in an economy in which the owners of means of production and the workers form distinct classes, and in which the dominant production relations are those of the sellers of labour power to the owners of means of production). But merchants exist in societies which are not all capitalist, and are not in the process of undergoing transition to capitalism. They may even perform vital functions in such pre-capitalist societies. In general, the behaviour of merchants in pre-capitalist societies is widely different from that of capitalists in developed capitalist societies. In developed capitalist societies, capitalists, generally with state support, play a very important part in modifying techniques of production and seeking ways of expanding their markets. By contrast, the pace of modification of techniques of production is generally much slower in pre-capitalist societies and owners of capital need not play a significant role in such modification.

Karl Marx recognized both the facts of integration of merchants in the pre-capitalist social structures in general, and their innovative role in developed capitalist societies. The canonical discussion of the role of merchants in pre-capitalist societies occurs in *Capital*, vol. III.[1] The discussion of the innovative role of capitalists occurs in *Theories of Surplus Value*.[2] In this latter passage, he describes the function of capitalists in inventing new methods of production of old substances, new substances, new uses for old substances, and diversifying the product-mix in general. But he associated such behaviour clearly with a developed capitalist economy, in which most of the population have been converted into wage earners, the tenant farmers have become industrial capitalists, and all property has assumed the form of easily negotiable capital.

Thus in Marx's analysis, it is not the subjective volition of individual merchants or capitalists, or even of groups of merchants or capitalists, but the nature of the societies in which they function that plays the predominant role in conditioning their behaviour. Of course, there is no impenetrable wall separating pre-capitalist from capitalist societies, nor is there an implication that the behaviour of the merchants or capitalists cannot influence the evolution of societies. In fact, it is the contradiction of the drives of an emerging capitalist class with a predominantly feudal society that was seen to constitute a major force for transition to capitalism. However, that contradiction must be coupled with other contradictions such as those of free peasants and feudal lords, or of yeoman farmers with landless labourers in order that the transition may actually occur.

Our aim here will be to analyse some of the ways in which merchants adjusted to British paramountcy. This will necessarily involve some discussion of the ways in which the merchants had interacted with pre-British socio-economic formations. The interaction would take the form of adjustment punctuated with incidents of conflict. The adjustment to British paramountcy would also take the form of both collaboration and conflict. But the nature of collaboration or conflict in the two epochs would generally differ.

Most analysts would agree in characterizing pre-British social formations in India as pre-capitalist formations. However, there are a hundred and one ways in which a mode of production or social formation can differ from capitalism. All the hundred and one ways are not viable and only some clusters might be actually observed. An even smaller number might have survival value in the sense of characterizing a recognizable social structure over a certain length of time. But these different clusters would provide their own environment for the formation of an identifiable and separate group of merchants and their survival as a separate group. When British colonialism brought the Indian economy under its sway, the pattern of interaction of mercantile capital with the rest of society would change, and correspondingly some changes would also take place in the internal organization of merchant communities and groups. One of the tasks of a historian of Indian society is to look at the process of selection of capitalists and the further processes of survival and growth or extinctions of particular mercantile groups. The current paper advances certain hypotheses which might help order the seemingly endless parade of mercantile groups across the pages of Mughal and British Indian history.

Some Salient Characteristics of Mercantile Groups in India in the Seventeenth and Eighteenth Centuries

Pre-British mercantile groups in India were enormously variegated in terms of ethnic and religious affiliation, connection with internal or external trade, the degree of diversification of functions, the scale of their operations, their connection with the actual processes of production and their propensity to collaborate with the British. There has been a considerable amount of work by economic and social historians in recent decades bearing on the fortunes of particular business communities in India. But practically the only works which look at the organization and behaviour of business communities in the British period across the whole of India and immediately before it are D.R. Gadgil's *Origins of the Modern Indian Business Class: An Interim Report*[3] and V.I. Pavlov's *Indian Capitalist Class*.[4] Gadgil's book, although shorter and less informative in many ways than Pavlov's, achieves a greater depth of analysis mainly because he is far more aware than Pavlov of the extremely vulnerable agrarian structure which provided the backdrop for the operations of

Indian merchants in pre-British times. By the vulnerability of the agrarian structure we mean (*a*) the high degree of susceptibility of crop output to fluctuations in weather conditions, (*b*) the near-subsistence level of living to which vast numbers of peasants, dependent labourers (including artisans), and wage labourers had been depressed, and (*c*) the huge drain of resources from agriculture to the urban areas. This vulnerability also provided opportunities for usury capital and speculative trading or banking capital by producing large fluctuations in harvest prices between seasons, years, and regions.[5] Pavlov's advantage lies in the use of an explicitly Marxist framework but his grasp of the material he handles is much less sure-footed than Gadgil's.[6]

The issues discussed in this paper were not central to Gadgil's pioneering study. Moreover, in some respects, I have benefited from the work of economic historians which was not available when Gadgil wrote his pioneering monograph. The major differences in our emphasis compared with his work may be summarized as follows: First, while Gadgil emphasizes the high degree of exploitation of cultivators and the largely one-way flow of surplus from the rural areas to towns under the Mughal (and post-Mughal) dispensations, he does not point out that this also provided an opportunity for making profit to the big bankers who supported the revenue-raising operations with advances to the landlords and rulers and the moneylenders who gave advances for subsistence to ordinary cultivators.[7] Second, as a corollary, Gadgil rather exaggerated the role of urbanization in the growth of business communities of India. Third, Gadgil paid little attention to the variety of ways in which merchants or bankers interacted with rulers in different parts of India. He underplayed both the importance of political patronage (and correspondingly, the opportunities available to *individual* merchants or particular business groups for acquiring political influence) for mercantile fortunes and the conflicts between merchants and rulers that broke out from time to time. Fourth, Gadgil fully accepted Van Leur's formulation that the distinction between 'pedlars' and 'merchant gentlemen' which was valid in the case of western Europe, say in the sixteenth or seventeenth centuries, did not apply to Asian traders. If this was just a question of a convenient classification of the activities and status of particular mercantile groups, an empirical refutation would suffice.[8] But this was also connected with Gadgil's implicit view that only individually large accumulations of capital devoted to specialized production mattered for economic growth.[9] Fifth, Gadgil tended to put more emphasis on formal guilds and associations of merchants and artisans and less emphasis on their informal modes of organization than the evidence about the power or influence of such guilds to withstand external pressure warrants. The power of sudden strikes or collective action on particular issues by merchants or artisans of a particular locality was probably as great or as little as that of organized associations in getting the rulers—indigenous or foreign—to change their policies or regulations. Finally, the strength of Gadgil's account—its lack of commitment to any rigid frame of analysis—is also a source of weakness. He fails to delineate how changes in the general structure of polity and society constrained or stimulated the activities of particular groups of merchants and traders.

We shall pay a good deal of attention to the ways in which Indian merchants adapted their behaviour in the face of British colonialism. In order to assess what constituted adaptive behaviour and what was simply a continuation of patterns evolved in pre-British times, it is necessary to have some idea of the typical pattern of behaviour in the earlier period. We have already posited that since the pre-British social formations were a good deal variegated, we would expect an enormous degree of variation in the organization, behaviour, and modes of interaction of mercantile communication. However, at the risk of being accused of perpetrating extreme oversimplification we shall pick out certain specific features of these three aspects, namely, the organization, behaviour, and modes of interaction (with the rulers as well as with the peasants and artisans) of important mercantile groups in pre-British times.

Merchants were organized in identifiable communities in most parts of India. There were big merchants, shipowners, or financiers such as Virjee Vora, Abdul Ghafur, or Fateh Chand Jagat Seth in Gujarat or Bengal. They were wealthy merchants on their own but they were identified as belonging to particular communities. There was considerable cross-communal cooperation in matters of business and other matters of common interest, and the governments often recognized heads of particular families (such as the family of Shantidas at Ahmedabad) or leaders of particular communities as spokesmen for the business community, the city, or particular sections of the business community, or particular localities of the city. Of course, there were business rivalries among prominent merchants, and sometimes these rivalries were given a specific communal colouring.[10] But there were many cases where business rivalries cut across any obvious communal lines or where different business groups cooperated in the face of a common threat.[11]

In some towns and cities, particularly in Gujarat, both merchants and artisans were organized in various associations or guilds.[12] The *mahajans* of merchants or the *panches* of artisans regulated commercial matters. Sometimes the caste *panchayat* and the mercantile or artisans *panchayat* were one and the same body, but this did not necessarily follow. Moreover, in some cities, such as Ahmedabad, the *Nagarseth* represented the city in crucial negotiations with rulers or invaders. Although these institutions were most prevalent and formally organized in Gujarat, *mahajan panchayats* and looser commercial associations, often cutting across caste barriers, have also been found in cities as widely dispersed as Poona, Murshidabad and Benares. The institutions of *Nagarseth*s and *panchayats* of merchants were widely prevalent in Rajasthan.[13]

There were, of course, different levels among the merchants and financiers. This is easiest to see in the case of the financiers. Some 'bankers' lent to the Mughal *subedars* or their successors—the local Nawabs or Rajas who grew up in different parts of India—and smaller *sahukars* lent to peasants, and artisans, and the smaller landlords. Similarly, the big merchants trading across the seas operated side by side with wholesale traders transporting goods from one region of the country to another, petty traders acting as procurement agents of the bigger merchants and, of course, shopkeepers and pedlars.

Since we are speaking about a rather ill-defined period roughly from the beginning of the seventeenth to the end of the eighteenth century—and since the information on any sub-period is rather fragmentary, it is not possible to make any generalization about the relative importance of seagoing merchants, big merchants of the interior, other wholesale merchants, and the vast numbers of petty traders who were engaged in mainly local trade. But it is important to emphasize the diversity of the organizational patterns, and the continued survival of vast numbers of independent small and not-so-small traders in various parts of the country. There were seagoing merchants owning a number of ships and dealing in millions of rupees, there were Bānjārās transporting vast quantities of grain and other produce from one part of the country to another, and there were *pykars*[14] or *byaparis* [traders or merchants] owning a number of pack animals or bullock-drawn carts transporting goods from one mart to another. The Armenians seem to have played a special role in linking different parts of India and the rest of middle and west Asia with India.[15] The Gujarati ship-owning merchants, particularly the Muslims among them, seem to have played a similar role in linking Bengal and Gujarat. The acquisition of political power by the (British) East India Company led to drastic decline in the fortunes of the Armenians and of the Gujarati merchants in Bengal.

When the Europeans came to trade in India, they adopted many of the features of the agency or *dālāli* [brokerage] system and the system of procurement through advances (*dādan*) that were practised by the Indian merchants. But wherever they could, they cut out the intermediaries and procured directly from the producers, or the small traders who acted as their agents. Many Indian intermediaries acting as collaborators of the foreigners were in fact ruined in the process. We shall deal with this issue a little later.

Most of the big Indian merchants dealt in a variety of commodities and often engaged in the retail trade (this might include local moneylending by big bankers). Most of the European companies also tried to procure a variety of goods for sale in Europe and for intra-Asian trade. As has been pointed out already, this was a rational policy in view of the enormous fluctuations and uncertainties of the markets in goods as well as in credit.

We come now to the behaviour of the merchants and their interaction with the rest of society and polity. The two themes are inextricably linked and we shall deal with them together.

The relations of bankers with ruling politicians are perhaps the simplest to describe. The bankers acted often as keepers of the state treasury and were often given the task of regulating the currency of the state.[16] They advanced money to the rulers when revenues fell short, or when the rulers (whether they were Mughal *subedars* or Maratha chieftains), needed money to finance their campaigns. In many cases, particularly in Rajasthan, the bankers also acted as tax farmers. The rulers sometimes relied on the bankers and the merchants for supply of essential commodities such as grain in times of scarcity and keeping prices down.[17]

Customs duties and other transit duties in ports were often collected by the rulers with the cooperation of leading merchants. Such reliance on Indian merchants or bankers apparently also extended to the Portuguese dependencies on the Indian soil.[18]

While it was not uncommon for the nobles or high officials of the Mughals to engage in commerce, anything more than a temporary interest, except in special cases, was either inconvenient or deliberately discouraged by the higher authority—particularly when it came to the superior office-holders. Thus Azim us-Shan, the grandson of Aurangzeb, was removed from the *subedari* of Bengal because he indulged excessively in private trade.[19] If it was unusual for nobles to become full-time merchants, it was also unusual for merchants to become nobles, particularly when their functions included military duties (Mir Jumla, of course, is an outstanding exception[20]). Big bankers and merchants could and did become ministers of kings and nawabs but, on the whole, it was understood that they would not aspire to membership of the class or group which ruled by the sword and by hereditary right. There are stories of kings and rulers confiscating the property of merchants or bankers, but they are mostly exaggerated. Sequestration of property on the death of a wealthy man seems to have been carried out mainly in the case of royal servants who were suspected of improper gain.[21]

Some of the big Muslim merchants (particularly in Gujarat) seem not to have obeyed the unwritten code of mutual forbearance between merchants and rulers, but they seem correspondingly to have suffered much more drastically than their Hindu counterparts when political fortunes changed.[22]

This code of mutual forbearance also applied to the relations between bankers or moneylenders and *zamindars* or owner-cultivators. There were occasions when *zamindari* rights changed hands because of indebtedness, but the transfers were probably limited within the circle who traditionally claimed rights of lordship. The transfer of ownership of cultivated land for indebtedness was rare: generally such transfers required the consent of village patels, *patidars*, or local *zamindars*. Evidence is accumulating, however, of more frequent transfers of land in the eighteenth century in Bengal and Rajasthan.[23] However, in Bengal, the Subarnabaniks, the traditional goldsmith and bullion dealing caste, are supposed to have desisted from purchases of land, and it is only the rising Telis or Gandhabaniks with interest in intra-village or intra-regional rather than inter-regional or riverine or coastal trade that were supposed to have deviated from the earlier mercantile code.[24]

These modes of interaction also went with typical modes of protest. The Chārans or Bhāts who acted as the carriers of Rajasthan (and later on, as Bānjārās, of most of northern and western India from Rajasthan to Mysore, on one side and the borders of Bihar, on the other) had a colourful mode of protest: they would threaten to commit suicide if their demands were not met.[25] Other merchants or artisans would resort to *hartals*; in extreme cases, merchants would threaten to desert a place en masse.[26] These protests were often quite effective because the purses of the rulers would be directly hit, and because they could not easily organize an alternative method of meeting the supply or credit requirements of people in their seats of power. Artisans and workers of various kinds as well as merchants could sometimes use their freedom to migrate, to break contracts and their collective organizations to make effective protests against extreme exploitation.[27] One of the distinguishing marks of British dominion in India was the relative ineffectiveness of such protests against rulers who were also merchants.

How did the merchants interact with the artisans? Although we do not know the quantitative significance of all the different possible modes of interaction between merchants and artisans, it is clear that the following patterns were widely observed: (a) The artisans often worked on their own, buying their own raw materials, working them up themselves, and selling them either to the nearby marts or to wholesale merchants (or their agents) who traded with other regions. (b) The artisan would be given an advance in money by the merchants. The former would buy the raw materials and deliver the product to the merchant at an agreed price. (c) The merchant would advance the raw materials to the artisan who would then deliver the finished or semi-finished product and would be paid at a piece-rate. In this case the artisan would essentially be reduced to the position of a wage labourer. (*d*) There were also manufactories in which a number of workers were brought together under one roof under the control of a merchant or merchants. But they were generally rare, for the reason that household-based industry allowed the merchant to expropriate the products of labour of all the members of the family, and no significant economies of scale seemed to operate in handicraft production. There were royal *kārkhānās* but they did not have to obey the dictates of the market.[28]

In later sections we shall refer back to some of these modes of interaction of merchants with the rest of society in pre-colonial India.

Influence of European Traders on Indian Merchants and Artisans before the Establishment of British Supremacy

Under the governorship of Afonso de Albuquerque, the Portuguese established themselves as the most powerful maritime power in the Arabian Sea and also in the eastern seas up to the Indonesian archipelago. They proceeded to utilize their position partly to monopolize the sea route to Europe round the Cape of Good Hope and partly to exact tributes from other seagoing merchants for 'protection' afforded to them. The Gujarati merchants initially offered stiff resistance against the depredations of the Portuguese, but after the 1530s, they generally accepted Portuguese control of the sea-lands and took out *cartazes* and paid duties to the Portuguese at Diu.[29] The Portuguese control over trade on the mainland was, however, extremely limited: they were fully occupied defending Goa and other mainland enclaves they had established.

With the coming of the Dutch in the seventeenth century, a new record was reached in ruthlessness and determination to monopolize trade. The attention of the Dutch East India Company came to be concentrated mainly on Indonesia and Ceylon. However, although their presence in India was limited to only a few settlements, they tried to control the channels of trade flowing into those points. For example, they tried to monopolize the trade between Hugli (in Bengal) and Ceylon.[30]

The Dutch were followed soon by the French and the English, and the ultimate tussle for supremacy in India and the surrounding seas lay between the French and the English. So

long as the Mughal power in India was intact,
neither of these trading companies could make
much headway in territorial conquests, but
that was not for want of trying. The English
were apt pupils of the Dutch who drove a hard
trade with the aid of armed ships and armies
where need be. The English came armed with
the notion that it was only with force and the
exercise of at least local sovereignty that they
could establish bases for trade, and it was
only by inspiring fear among the Asians that
they could overcome the obduracy of the
local rulers.[31]

How far did the operations of the European
companies and private traders (including
'interlopers') lead to the enrichment of Indian
merchants and artisans? The enrichment could
come about through an expansion of the output
of Indian fields and cottages because of the
stimulus provided by expanding trade, through a
rise in the share obtained by the merchants and
artisans of a constant retained value of the
articles exported, or through an increase in the
prices of the articles exported in comparison
with those of imported articles. The evidence
on all these aspects is as yet fragmentary. It
has sometimes been claimed, mainly on the
basis of the records of the European trading

companies, that total exports of India increased significantly in the seventeenth or eighteenth centuries. Even the records of the trading companies do not show an unambiguous trend. For example, the total imports from Asia into Britain on account of the English East India Company reached a value of £802,527 in 1684 and remained well below that figure until 1741; in fact, it is doubtful whether any increasing trend in the figures could be established between 1684 and 1760 (when the figure of imports was £711,340).[32]

It is possible that increasing exports to other regions of India by the European companies were the dynamic element in the export trade. But on that score also the evidence is not unambiguous; a part, probably a major part, of the increase attained by the European companies was at the cost of the Asian merchants, and there occurred significant diversions of trade as between Asia and Europe and as between different Asian regions. The evidence regarding the terms of exchange between imports and exports as a whole remains equally ambiguous.

But what is not ambiguous is that the European companies meant to engross the major part of the gains that accrued from intra-Asian maritime trade and from trade between India and Europe. Their control of the sea lanes to Europe and the total exclusion of Indian merchants from access to markets in Europe or to sources of supply of the few commodities (including bullion) that were brought from west of Arabia to India gave the European companies a decisive advantage over the Indian merchants.[33]

Of course, the Europeans were not content with domination of the sea lanes, or the markets in Europe. They also wanted to exercise monopolistic control over supplies of the exportables in India. Where their political presence was feeble, their ability to subordinate Indian merchants was of a low order, but they had a good try nevertheless, and many merchants were ruined in the process of trading with them.[34] In a situation of widely fluctuating markets and large cash requirements for working capital and for advances to suppliers, small merchants are often ruined in the course of dealing with big bankers and merchants.[35] But the European companies were often in the position of borrowers in relation to the Indian merchants. It is essentially the political power wielded by the European companies that enabled them to subordinate their Indian suppliers—both merchants and artisans—and drive many Indian merchants out of business in the process or ruin or impoverish them financially.

Thus, for example, the English East India Company was much more effective in organizing 'joint stocks' of supplying merchants subordinate to them in Madras at a time when their attempts to do so in Bengal were as yet unsuccessful, because they exercised more complete local sovereignty at Fort St George than at Calcutta before the Battle of Plassey.[36]

Finally, there is no evidence whatever that artisans obtained a larger share of the value of the produce when they supplied the goods produced (either directly or through intermediaries) to the European trading companies.

The Fate of Independent Merchants and Artisans in the Areas of Colonial Control

The direct imposition of colonial control blocked certain avenues of development of both mercantile groups and artisanal work in the eighteenth and nineteenth centuries. In the context of Europe, Marx noted that there was a three-fold transition from merchant capital or artisanal industry to industrial capital:

First, the merchant becomes directly an industrial capitalist. This is true in crafts based on trade, especially crafts producing luxuries and imported by merchants together with the raw materials and labourers from foreign lands, as in Italy from Constantinople in the 15th century. Second, the merchant turns the small masters into his middlemen, or buys directly from the independent producer, leaving him nominally independent and his mode of production unchanged. Third, the industrialist becomes merchant and produces directly for the wholesale market.[37]

In the same chapter, he characterized the third path of transition as 'the really revolutionising way.' Whether Marx's statement can be applied in the same way to Germany, Russia, or Japan, as to Britain, France, or the USA and whether any distinctions in this regard pick out the countries undergoing a bourgeois-democratic revolution from those in which such revolutions had to await their defeat by foreign countries or were rendered unnecessary by a socialist revolution are questions we will not debate in this paper. What is obvious is that the last two modes of translation described by Marx were practically never observed in India or in other third world countries. Modern industrialists arose from the ranks of merchants who initially imported the needed techniques and methods of organization from abroad with some local adaptations.

One of the reasons for the failure of the third or even the second mode of transition in India was that the operation of colonialism initially decimated the ranks of independent artisans or merchants who had close links with production of craft industries. The change brought about by colonialism in this respect can be easily seen by comparing the situation of independent merchants and artisans at the end of the eighteenth century in Bengal and in Tipu Sultan's Mysore soon after the British had conquered that state. (Information about the latter state is available from the reports of Francis Buchanan who was sent by the East India Company to survey the resources of the conquered territories.[38])

If we look at the situation of merchants and artisans in eighteenth-century British Bengal, then several patterns of life cycles of merchants as traders on their own, merchants as middlemen between artisans and European chartered companies or private traders, merchants as putters-out, merchants as employers of wage labour, and of artisans as independent producers, artisans acting as production agents of merchants or European companies, artisans as wage labourers in their own crafts and artisans turning into landless agricultural or general labourers can be seen. A typical sequence was as follows: The East India Company buys cotton or silk goods from middlemen; after a few seasons it puts pressure on the middlemen to cut down prices either by rejecting goods supplied as substandard or by refusing payment to them for the full quota; the middlemen are ruined or retreat from the market; the Company moves in to give advances to the artisans directly or through *dalāls* and binds the artisans not to sell their goods to competitors; the artisans are effectively reduced to mere wage earners or worse; since peons are posted on them for the collection of the finished goods and they are arrested and molested in other ways if they fail to comply with the legal or illegal demands of the Company's servants; then the external market for the goods purchased by the Company collapses; the latter refuses to buy goods in former volumes; the artisans are in turn ruined; and either hang on precariously to their earlier occupations or become general labourers looking for any employment (since few of the artisans owned land).

The developments in the various spheres of production up to the beginning of the 1780s and the fates of the Indian merchants and producers connected with them were brilliantly summed up in Burke's *Ninth Report*.[39] The trade in cotton cloth formed the major staple of the Company's investments, and here the heavy-handed coercion of the Company and its servants was felt perhaps by the largest number of direct producers. The *dadni* merchants or agents of the Company suffered in their turn as the Company changed its policy. The merchants or agents, of course, tried to transmit the pressure down to the weavers, generally successfully.

Trade in salt, over which the pre-British rulers had exercised only a loose kind of monopoly, was brought under a rigorous monopoly by Clive's Society of Trade. When this monopoly was abolished, and production and trade were thrown open to other traders subject to the payment of a duty, the Company's servants managed to corner most of the trade.[40] There were numerous turnabouts in the policy regarding salt, but the Company always retained monopoly rights in its trade. Salt production had been organized earlier by Indian merchants and *zamindars* and produced by a class of producers called *molungees* [proprietors or renters of salt pans]. Under the dispensation of the Company, the supervision (and profits) of production devolved either on the Company's servants or salt farmers who were often *benamis* of those servants, and the oppression of the *molungees* probably increased as the Company sought to fix prices as well as quantities of salt to be delivered by the *Jattar*.

In the case of silk production one of the earliest moves of the Company was to discourage the production of finished silk goods, often by using force, since it was found to be more profitable to export silk yarn. In an attempt to improve the spinning and reeling methods, the Company promoted the introduction of Italian silk filatures.[41] Many Indian merchants (including substantial ryots) set up filatures on their own. Filatures were also set up by *pykars* who acted as the middlemen between the *chassars* (the cocoon rearers) and the East India Company or other buyers of raw silk.

However, in order to prevent silk yarn from being sold to rival European Companies or traders or Indian merchants trading with other parts of India, the East India Company tried to compulsorily rent or buy up the filatures belonging to *pykars* or to independent Indian producers. These measures naturally led to conflicts. However, from the end of the 1820s onwards a decisive decline in demand for silk yarn and silk goods set in, and many independent producers gave up the production of yarn and voluntarily turned into agents for procurement of the Company's cocoons or raw silk.

Similar stories can be told of the suppliers of most of the other items of 'investment', such as opium or saltpetre in which the East India Company was interested. Against the relentless pressure of the English East India Company to monopolize the trade in all the items it was interested in, the Indian merchants and middlemen had three escape routes. The first was the opportunity for trading with other European Companies or traders.[42]

Apart from the French and Danish Companies, there were the private European traders who operated legally or illegally within the Company's territory, and who provided some competition against the English East India Company. The Company's servants also traded on the side and connived with their Indian collaborators in evading some of the regulations of the Company. But the Napoleonic Wars saw the disappearance of

French competition, although they at the same time stimulated 'smuggling' and 'interloping'.

The second escape route available to the Indian merchants and the producers was sale to the home market, including the other regions of India. However, the scope for such sales became more restricted as the Company took increasingly effective measures to eliminate the competition of the Armenian and other merchants trading with the other parts of India and as the incomes of Indian consumers—of both luxury goods and necessities—declined as a result of policies adopted by the Company. The tariff policy of the Company, of course, compounded the problem.[43] Smuggling of salt and of opium could also be treated as exploitation of the Indian home market by the Indian merchants (sometimes in collusion with the Company's servants) in a situation where the Company left no room for the legitimate activities of the independent merchants.[44]

The third escape route for the Indian merchants and middlemen was to pass the pressure down to the producers. This took the form of binding the producers by giving them advances (*pykars* and salt farmers resorted to this extensively), of using actual physical force or the threat of physical coercion, and the invoking of the authority of the Company to browbeat the producers. Debt bondage was an extremely effective device because of the inexorable revenue demands of the Company—a demand that was rarely abated for famines, floods, droughts or other natural calamities.[45] Thus the Company in effect imposed a mutually reinforcing policy of exploitation for grinding the primary producers—artisans and cultivators alike—down to the subsistence level.

The direct producers, naturally, had much fewer escape routes. So long as the custom of rival traders was available, they could try to elude the control of the Company. The producers of handloom cloth would produce for the local market. But the producers of luxury goods or exportables did not have much of a home market to fall back on.

In the face of all these pressures, there were naturally protests and collective resistance. The handloom weavers of Santipore in Bengal put up a determined resistance against the constant attempt at price-cutting by the Company.[46] Salt merchants combined with local *zamindars* to frustrate the attempts of salt farmers to control the trade as authorized by the Company, and carried on a thriving trade in contraband salt.

Such resistance was, of course, sought to be put down by the Company with the use of force, but where there was an internal market for the commodity, new 'smugglers' grew up to take the place of older merchants.

Sometimes the protest by the artisans took the form of giving up the calling altogether, as happened with the makers of *tanjeebs* [a fine variety of muslin] at Teetabaddy in the Dacca district.[47] Increasingly, of course, as the forces of de-industrialization released by the Company's industries and advent of machine-made goods from Europe overwhelmed the country, more and more merchants and producers lost their capital or their means of livelihood and were pushed back to the land as cultivators or as landless agricultural workers. *Pykars* or independent merchants of silk who had earlier advanced money to the Company or other buyers of their goods now had to seek advances from the Company in order to meet their revenue and other cash obligations.[48] Many artisans who had earlier worked on their own became dependent on moneylenders for financing their requirements of raw materials and subsistence. In northern India, handloom weavers broke out in violent disturbances again and again as the forces of de-industrialization swept over them. For example, at Mubarakpur in the Azamgarh district of Uttar Pradesh, between 1813 and 1841, *julahas* [weavers] broke out in several cases in violent riots, the major target of their wrath being the moneylenders.[49] Throughout the nineteenth century, there were many movements of artisans as well as peasants in which moneylenders were singled out as targets of attack.

Even in post-Plassey Bengal, some Indian merchants prospered. But few of them prospered as independent merchants. Most of them owed their position directly or indirectly to the protection of powerful servants of the East India Company, such as Clive, Hastings, Vansittart, Verelst, or later on, to their collaboration with European business houses such as Palmer & Co., Alexander & Co., or Mackintosh & Co. They might be called *banians*, *sarkars*, or *dewans*. We shall use the generic epithet *banian* for all of them.[50] The servants of the East India Company needed them as fronts for their illegal trading operations, as go-betweens for collecting information or bribes, as their channels of information on the Indian environment, and often as the initial providers of capital.

But the need of the Europeans for the services of these Indian collaborators diminished as the East India Company gave up its trading monopoly, so that private European capitalists could trade on their own in an unrestricted fashion, and as the Europeans acquired a better grip over the local money market through the floating of banks such as the Bank of Bengal, Union Bank, and the Agra and United Services Bank. Furthermore, as European capital was directed towards indigo and sugar plantations and to the importing of manufactures rather than to the export of products of Indian craft industry, and as British control over the hinterland increased, the dependence of the Europeans on their Indian partners diminished very greatly.

In order to understand what happened to the fabulously wealthy Bengali *banians* or *dewans* of the East India Company's servants or its various departments (for example, Dwarkanath Tagore was *dewan* of the Salt Department),[51] it may be useful to divide this class of people into two broad groups: those who had made their money before 1800 or so, and those who made it afterwards. Most of the *banians* who made their money before 1800 as associates of the servants of the Company had easy opportunities of investing it in landed property. For example, Gokul Ghosal, the *banian* of

Verelst, and the founder of the Bhukailas Raj family, was a big trader and a farmer of revenues. He and his nephew, Joynarayan Ghosal, acquired landed property and the family joined the ranks of the leading *zamindars* of Bengal.[52] The same thing happened with the senior (Pathuriaghata) branch of the Tagore family.

The families which remained closely connected with the leading European agency houses or tried to compete with them in the usual export trades were less lucky. The Burrals, who were *banians* of Alexander & Co. for at least two generations went down when that firm closed its doors in 1832. The collapse of handloom exports of Bengal and the crisis in the indigo trade in the late 1820s and the 1830s brought down not only the leading agency houses and their close associates but also such leading Indian firms as Mathooramohun Sein & Co. Only those Indians whose fortunes could not be forfeited as belonging to nominal partners of European agency houses and who managed to create some substantial property in land or real estate escaped the holocaust of the 1830s. The fall of the Union Bank merely marked the end of a process which had begun much earlier; the defaulting European merchants decamped with the money or passed practically unscathed through the portals of the courts as insolvent debtors while their Indian *banians* and partners were sold up for the debts of the firms. It is symptomatic that Dwarkanath's knowledge of the law and his foresight, in putting his *zamindaris* in trust for his sons saved his *zamindari* property from the debtors, while his business was wound up on his death.[53]

The question as to why the Parsi or Gujarati collaborators of Europeans in Bombay survived as businessmen has been raised and answered in different ways. No really full answer can be given until we have as much scholarly work available on the trade and economy of the Bombay Presidency in the early part of the nineteenth century as we have on Bengal. I have argued elsewhere that a major part of the explanation lies in the earlier and more complete domination of the hinterland of Calcutta as compared with that of Bombay, by the British.[54] In elaboration of that argument, I would add that since the Maratha Confederacy was not finally defeated until 1818, and the East India Company lost its trading monopoly between Europe and India in 1813, the merchants and artisans of western India escaped the worst excesses of the coercive monopoly imposed by the East India Company and its servants. The British often needed the help of the Parsis in their wars against the Marathas and the Parsis were eager to follow the British in establishing trading connections, particularly in China and East Africa. At least until the British had acquired unchallenged political supremacy in that part of India, these factors enabled the Parsi merchants to secure more of a semblance of equality with their European partners.

The types of products exported from western India in the early part of the nineteenth century also offered certain advantages to the Indian merchants. Both cotton and opium came from deep inside the hinterland, often from areas which were within native states and which were relatively inaccessible until the advent of the railways. The British never succeeded in completely controlling the production and trade in Malwa opium, in contrast to their monopolization of opium production and trade in eastern India. The same thing is true of trade in cotton, which was produced by millions of peasants. It would appear that in the first part of the nineteenth century (at least until 1851 or so) most of the internal trade in cotton in western India had passed from the hands of the Europeans who probably found it more profitable to concentrate on external trade.[55] Moreover, the export trade in neither of these crops experienced a crisis of a magnitude that occurred in the case of exports of cotton cloth, silk goods or indigo in eastern India.[56]

On the negative side, collaborators of British officials never had the opportunity for acquiring revenue farming rights that new *babus* and rajas of Bengal enjoyed in the later part of the eighteenth century and the early part of nineteen century.

However, the survival of Indian merchants with a toehold in big-time export trade in the early nineteenth century did not necessarily guarantee that they would be the first group of Indians to invest on a large scale in modern manufacturing industry. The Indian merchants in western India obtained a new lease of life from the cotton boom of 1862–5, and then the enormous profitability of the pioneer cotton mills in Bombay showed them the way to the future.[57] Indian merchants were eliminated in the financial crisis of 1865–7; however, the holocaust was smaller than that which overtook the Indian merchants of Calcutta in the aftermath of the agency house collapses of 1830–4 for three reasons: (*a*) The majority of Indian mercantile houses in Bombay were by then trading on their own, and they did not have to pay the debts of their British counterparts. (*b*) An insolvency law passed obligingly by the Bombay Government made it very difficult for creditors to get hold of the property of the insolvent debtors. (*c*) Since most Bombay merchants were governed by the Mitāksharā system of inheritance laws, it was difficult for creditors to sell up the property of the defaulting debtors.

Even apart from the financial crisis of 1865–7, the Indian mercantile community of Bombay was exposed to other forces tending to undermine their position vis-à-vis European houses. First of all, the extension of railway communications into the interior enabled European export houses such as Ralli Bros., Volkart Bros., etc. to penetrate directly into the cotton districts and eliminate the smaller Indian merchants. The acquisition of the cotton-rich Berar districts by the British Government from the Nizam in the 1850s gave the British firms a far easier access to those districts. Furthermore, the large-scale operations of the big European export houses enabled them to reap the advantages of technology that was complementary to railway carriage. At first, the cotton crop was sent in loosely packed *dokras*, or rough sacks; their bulk made it impossible for the Great Indian Peninsula Railway to carry them off to the ports promptly. Then presses and half-presses were set up for packing cotton into fully pressed and half-pressed bales. The railways conferred an advantage on owners of full presses by charging a higher freight rate on half-pressed bales.[58] Naturally, big export houses controlling large numbers of presses in the cotton districts came to enjoy an enormous advantage over the majority of Indian cotton exporters.

The spread of European-dominated financial institutions also tended to favour the big merchants with Presidency-wide connections in relation to the smaller merchants, and European merchants in relation to the Indians. When the (old) Bank of Bombay opened a branch at Broach, it favoured the Europeans and Eurasians at the expense of the Indian dealers so that the Bombay Gazetteer recorded in 1877 that the greater part of the cotton trade was by then 'carried on by Europeans and Eurasians, only about one-eighth remaining in the hands of the local capitalists'.[59] Similarly, in the district of Khandesh, it was reported in 1880 that with improved communications local moneylenders and traders had been worsted by Marwari merchants and Bhatias from Bombay (the latter were said to be 'masters of the new system of trade by rail and wire'), and the trade at Jalgaon was then mostly in the hands of nineteen firms, two of them European—the Mofussil and the New Berar Companies.[60]

The upshot of all this was that the Europeans apparently managed to acquire a much larger share of the cotton trade in 1875 compared with 1851.[61] However, in spite of the changes, Indians did manage to retain a significant share in cotton exports. The British Government was also not able to bring the export of Malwa opium entirely under its control, and Indian traders had a freer hand in the native states from which this opium came than in British territory. However, what really saved the Indian mercantile community in western India was the growth of cotton mills in Bombay and Ahmedabad. Most of the merchants setting up these mills continued to have a large stake in trade as well as industry, and the pattern has continued till today.

The Absolutism of Tipu versus Capitalist Colonialism

Our comparison between Indian merchants in eastern India and in Bombay or Gujarat has at best been incomplete. In particular, we have said little about the fate of artisans in Bombay proper, mainly because I am not familiar with the material available on the subject. But incomplete as it is, we have seen that it is possible to discuss the fates of the *babu* collaborators of Calcutta and the *saheb* collaborators of Bombay without postulating *ab initio* that it was the difference in their values or even their life styles which led to the difference in their fates. There were definite differences in the aspirations of the Parsi *sahebs* and the Bengali *babus*. The former wanted to be esquires, knights and baronets, the latter were satisfied with the titles of Rajas and Maharajas.[62] The Bengali *babus* probably were more inward-looking, valuing the accolade given by the larger, tradition-bound society more than the Parsis did, for the simple reason that the latter belonged to a small community which had prospered with migration from Surat to Bombay, and had therefore no larger community to seek approbation from. An enlightened *babu* such as Dwarkanath Tagore might endow the Calcutta Medical College or start steamship companies, and might yet spend an enormous sum on alms to Brahmans on the death of his adoptive mother. On the other side of India, Ardeshir Cursetjee Wadia, the first Indian to be elected a Fellow of the Royal Society, even when travelling to England with the object of improving his skills as a mechanical engineer, would refuse to eat cooked food if it had not been prepared by a Parsi.[63] In respect of expenditure for entertaining the Europeans, there was probably not much to choose between the two groups of collaborators. The Bengali *babus* almost certainly wasted more money on ceremonies without getting any financial return. But such wasteful expenditure was at least partly the result of the blocking of their investment opportunities. Most of the differences in the fortunes of the two communities can be explained by the greater degree of independence from individual Europeans acquired by Parsi merchants such as Jamsetji Jejeebhoy, Framjee Cowasjee, etc. and by the easier access they enjoyed to external trade. The study of differences in such objective factors caused by the differential impact of colonialism has to go much further before we need to bring in differences in world outlooks to explain the differences in the fates of Bengali *banians* and Parsi guarantee brokers.

We have already seen, by comparing Mughal and British India, that the political power acquired by the British East India Company had a significant impact on the fortunes and position of Indian merchants and artisans. Interestingly enough, colonialism can be seen to have had a decisive impact even compared with the kind of absolutist state Tipu Sultan sought to set up in Mysore. Tipu's government had a monopoly of trade in sandalwood, black pepper, and cardamom. It engaged in foreign trade on a large scale and it sought to engross some sectors of the wholesale trade.[64] Some measures of Tipu's government—such as prohibition of trade with British-controlled territories—were almost certainly dictated by his inimical relations with the East India Company's government and by the continual tendency of the merchants to evade some of the regulations.

These measures of Tipu may have alienated some of the bigger merchants, but many artisans, employers of wage labour, and smaller merchants seem to have prospered under his reign. Production by artisans on the basis of advances made by merchants was also very widespread in his Kingdom. Francis Buchanan bears ample testimony to this. The iron smelting enterprises in Mysore generally approximated to the employment of artisans as wage labourers by proprietors. Buchanan found the apparent profit remaining to the proprietor to be rather small (this was true of iron smelting in the districts of Madhu-giri, Chin-narayan-durga, Hagalawadi and Devaraya-durga). He concluded that the proprietor in general got the money from the merchant, and that 'his only claim for reward [was] some trouble in settling the accounts and the risk of some of the people running away with the advances made to them.'[65]

At Sati-mangalam (on the way from Kaveri-pura Ghat to Coimbatore) Buchanan found weavers taking advances from Indian merchants as well as from the Commercial Resident of the East India Company at Saliem (Salem).[66] His view was that the Indian merchants kept the weavers always in debt; so long as the weaver was indebted to a merchant, he must always work for him at a low rate; and if a merchant wanted to take a new weaver in employ, he must repay the latter's debt to his former master. But in the same district Buchanan found weavers rich enough to make the cloth on their own account, and sell it to the best advantage.

At Coimbatore, which had earlier been within Tipu's kingdom, Buchanan found weavers either taking advances from Indian merchants, or producing cloth with their own capital:

> Each of the different classes of weavers here forming, as it were, a kind of family, the richer assist the poor; so that those who work for country use are either able to make the cloth on their own account, or at least are not obliged to take advances from a native merchant for more than one piece at a time. Those who once get into the debt of a native merchant are ever afterwards little better than slaves, and must work for him at a low rate.

Even under Tipu, thus, handicraftsmen could not entirely avoid the fate of debt-slavery to merchants.[67] Moreover, Tipu's kingdom was, after 1792, a beleaguered fortress, constantly under threat of British occupation. Also, in spite of his attempts to shut out the evil influence of the British traders, the artisans and merchants were subjected to the pull of their export-oriented business connections. Subject to all these limitations, artisans and merchants retained a considerable degree of independence, particularly when they catered to the home market: Tipu's policies were at least not designed to contract the size of that market. In fact, some of his policies went further in diffusing new skills—such as those of metal work and gun-making, and stimulating local production. British policies and the influence of the international capitalist network could only thwart artisanal production and mercantile independence. At Sati-mangalam, for example, Buchanan found that many weavers had given up working in protest against a stamp-duty on the amount of cloth produced which had replaced a tax on looms that Tipu had levied (the latter would, *ceteris paribus*, stimulate output).

Over the course of the nineteenth century, the handloom industry remained far more intact in south India than in most other parts of India. The relative inaccessibility of much of the terrain, the consumption habits of the people, the local supplies of cotton, the desperately low standard of living of the handicraftsmen (and labourers in general) may all have contributed to this outcome. But it is worth asking how much Tipu's desperate stand against the British till the very end of the eighteenth century was responsible for this outcome. While Tipu's government tried to monopolize trade in certain articles, most internal trade was left free, and encouragement was also offered to specific (generally non-British) groups of merchants or individuals for trading with his kingdom.[68] Further, in the trading corporation set up by Tipu's state, ordinary subjects could take a share.[69] Thus Tipu's monopoly was of a very different kind from the one imposed by the East India Company and private European merchants in Bengal between 1757 and 1813. Moreover, the encouragement of production of new types of goods, including armaments and metal products, mainly for internal use, also provided stimulus to both artisanal and mercantile activity. Some of the mercantile groups which thrived under Tipu's dispensation somehow survived in the truncated state of Mysore and helped slow down the process of de-industrialization and the European monopolization of mercantile activity in the interior of south India. But these suppositions need to be substantiated by intensive work on the transition in Tipu's kingdom and the native state of Mysore under British protection.

Artisans as well as merchants were all the time at risk when faced with the deliberate weapons and the impersonal forces released by colonialism. But there were some areas less at risk than others. A greater degree of organization among merchants and artisans probably did increase their power of resistance against colonial depredations. Gujarati merchants, as we shall see, made a better showing in this respect than most other mercantile communities.

Gujarati artisans seem also to have shared some of this relative immunity. Even as late as the latter part of the nineteenth century, we have accounts of artisans in Gujarat who were themselves men of some capital. For example among the Bhavsars—calico-printers and dyers by profession—there were men of capital who owned from Rs 5,000 to Rs 20,000 and prepared articles on their own account. But the majority seem to have been employed by traders and 'other men of capital' and were paid according to the number of robes or *saris* they printed.[70]

In order that merchants should be able to control production and accumulate capital on that basis, the craft organization of production itself must survive, and must prove a profitable avenue for employment of capital. For master craftsmen to become industrial capitalists, the same condition must apply and in addition, the craftsmen must be prosperous enough to accumulate capital for investment in increasingly capital-intensive enterprises.[71] In colonial India, it was the merchants who emerged as industrial capitalists because artisans were too poor, and because many of them had been thrown out of craft employment through processes of de-industrialization. But in the rare cases where craft production survived, it did provide a reservoir of skills for some branches of modern industry. Thus in Gujarat, the craft skills of bleaching and dyeing proved useful for mill production of cotton cloth.[72] In England, skills of woodworking were often transferable to the fabrication of the early vintages of machines with wooden as well as metal parts.[73]

The survival of clusters of merchants and artisans moving jointly into the machine age was practically ruled out in most parts of British India. Even Gujarat provides only a partial exception. The only link between the craft skills and machine industry was often provided by the *julahas* or *tantis* manning the weaving departments of jute mills and cotton mills: this generally meant only a transition from semi-servile wage earners in craft industry to semi-servile wage labourers in mill barracks.

Conditions for Survival of Mercantile Communities in Nineteenth-Century India

While independent artisans practically disappeared from the face of the Indian earth, some mercantile communities survived to provide the controllers of large business houses in twentieth-century India. Given the fact that after 1818, no major part of India was outside British political hegemony, what were the conditions for survival of the mercantile communities? Without presuming to provide an exhaustive answer to such a question, the following four sets of factors may be singled out for special attention. First, the relationship of merchants to land was crucial in determining whether they would be wiped out in a major depression when they were not backed by the security of land, or whether they would find a mode of survival as merchants by diversifying into the control of the usufruct of land while remaining merchants. Second, and connected with the first set of factors, the continued existence of numerous native principalities provided a limited sanctuary to some groups of bankers against the worst imposts of British rule. Third, the laws relating to inheritance seem to have been very important in preserving or destroying mercantile property. Paradoxically enough, the communities under the more 'progressive' (because more individualistic) system were wiped out whereas those who survived were all under some variant of the 'less progressive' system of Mitākṣharā law. Fourth, only those mercantile communities survived which managed to retain an intra-communal cohesiveness as merchants. In a sense, the community had to be semi-open and dense in terms of organizational network. It had to be capable of digesting intelligence regarding changes in the patterns of trade and reacting to it appropriately; at the same time it had to have chains of communication and trade which could not be disrupted by competitors from outside.

Land and the Indian Mercantile Community

In pre-British India, by and large, private property in land was hedged in by various restrictions imposed by the superior political authority or by local communities. Superior rights to the produce of the land in the form of a right to share in the rent went with claims to a position within the political hierarchy.[74] Right to cultivate the land, on the other hand, belonged to the peasants or ryots whose movement was sought to be limited by various devices. Merchants did not fit into either of these categories. In Gujarat the Hindu merchants shared with the common (non-Rajput) peasantry the characteristic of being unarmed[75] and with the ruling princes or mercenary soldiers that of having no special restrictions on mobility. But they had to seek the protection of controllers of land, be they Mughal princes or *subedars*, Rajput or Maratha kings or chieftains, or autochthonous tribes.[76] The inability of the merchants to fight oppression politically, which has been commented on, has something to do with this enforced disarmament of the mercantile community—particularly among the Hindus.[77]

The introduction by the British of generalized private property in land and the effective separation of landownership from the right to share in the formal political decision-making[78] changed all this. But the changes were by no means complete nor of a uniform character in all parts of India.

When the British laws, aimed at making land a vendible commodity and abolishing most of the traditional restrictions on the alienation of land for debt, were introduced, certainly more merchants and moneylenders began to acquire land than they had ever done before. But in most parts of India, merchants or moneylenders did not corner the major fraction of the land that changed hands, nor did they rush in to buy land or revenue-farming rights wherever an opportunity presented itself.[79]

There were certain obstacles against merchants turning landlords in British India. First, the purchase of land renders capital illiquid so that the merchant is not able to take advantage of more profitable opportunities of investing it, should they be available in future. The more localized and the more imperfect the market in land or in superior rights to land, the greater is the illiquidity or immobility of capital invested in landownership or revenue farming. The difficulty of communication between different parts of the country before the spread of the railways all over India and the existence of overlapping rights in the same piece of land held by several persons meant that land was both an imperfect and, from a financial (and not just physical) point of view, an immobile asset.[80]

The second obstacle in the way of merchants becoming landholders was that the British did not really convert land into a fully vendible commodity. For political reasons, they had to recognize, at least in the region outside Bengal, that there were several layers of claims to the same piece of land, so that an unambiguous property in land could not be created. Moreover, no land could be held by a proprietor absolutely (except in Assam or other plantation areas where the British introduced the right of holding land under a 'free simple' tenure for the benefit of European planters). The regular payment of rent or tax to the government was the condition for holding any piece of land, and the governmental claim in this respect overrode the claims of all other creditors. In the permanently settled areas of Bengal, the British Government perhaps came closest to ignoring the rights of the inferior right holders and peasants, and it is not surprising that many wealthy merchants bought *zamindari* rights there. However, even in Bengal it would be wrong to say that merchants became *zamindars* and therefore ceased to be merchants. It would be more appropriate to say that with the drying up of investment opportunities and the extreme vulnerability of exports of traditional commodities, prudence dictated that a substantial part of the wealth, however acquired, should be invested in *zamindari*, urban real estate or government securities. In fact, many wealthy merchant families by and large avoided *zamindari* (whose management was not within the range of skills expected of a traditional merchant) and invested their wealth in the other two kinds of assets.[81]

The third obstacle against merchants turning into landowners was the existence of strong *zamindars* (persons recognized from pre-British days as possessing the right to pay government revenue) or *taluqdars* or their equivalents on the land and their resistance against the attempt of an outsider or a local new man to exercise superior right in land.

In the *ryotwari* areas, these difficulties were compounded by another factor. The cost of managing a large number of scattered holdings could be quite high, so that a really big merchant or banker would not find it profitable to lock a substantial part of his capital in land. Moreover, the government probably appropriated a much larger fraction of the surplus produced by *ryotwari* land, so that the attractiveness of revenue farming was lower than the permanently settled areas. Also, in the latter parts of the country, the surplus according to the *zamindar* or the holders of intermediary rights tended to go up with population growth, growth of output, and increase in the proportion of marketed to total output. The *ryotwari* area on the other hand probably enjoyed a higher rate of growth of agricultural productivity.[82] The merchant could often extract a higher surplus from the peasant by keeping him in debt bondage and sequestering part of his produce every year than by taking the land away from him.

The factors mentioned above would go a long way to explain why many important mercantile groups remained merchants and did not become landed magnates. There are even cases recorded of merchants who wanted to retain an 'image of the "*accommodating saraf*"', by lending money to *zamindars* at high rates of interest, but without acquiring a permanent title to land.[83] Of course, when opportunity beckoned, merchants were not backward in acquiring *zamindari* rights cheaply, particularly if the firm was big enough to consider such purchases as just a way of spreading risks as between different assets in its portfolio. Thus several large Marwari firms, which had been generally reluctant to hold illiquid assets, became big *zamindars* in Uttar Pradesh owning scores of villages each.[84] Moreover, for the sake of prestige (which might not be without its commercial value), a branch of the family might become landlords, or describe themselves as *zamindars*.[85] However, too close an involvement in landownership and management generally meant the doom of the family as merchants.

Because of peasant resistance and fear of ruin of old *zamindar* and *taluqdar* families, the British Government, from the 1870s onwards, interposed legal obstacles against the acquisition of land or *zamindari* rights by 'non-agriculturists' in the Bombay Presidency, United Provinces, and Punjab. This did not, of course, stop transfers of land to merchants or bankers under various pretexts or disguises nor did it stop the so-called 'agriculturists' themselves turning into usurers vis-a-vis declining or extravagant *zamindars* and seasonally or chronically starving peasants. Hence in order to analyse the peculiar amalgam of methods of exploitation through usury, landlordism, and monopsony in trade, we have to study the phenomenon of the landlord acting as usurer and trader as closely as that of the merchant or banker turning into a landlord. Even where the landlord was the main exploiter, the merchant was often a crucial servicing agent to the mechanism of exploitation. He supplied funds to the *zamindar* regularly or in emergencies,[86] he helped market the produce retained by the *zamindar* or sold in distress by the peasants, and he lent money to the peasantry and kept them in thralldom, often acting as an agent of the *zamindar*. There were many conflicts between the *zamindar* and the merchant but such conflicts did nothing to change the mechanism of exploitation.

What I have said underscores the fact that many old mercantile houses in the interior of India must have seen their role, even under British rule, as a continuation of their earlier function of servicing the mechanism of tribute extraction by the landed magnates rather than supplanting them. At least this must have been true in the first half of the nineteenth century in those areas where the rights of the so-called village *zamindars* or village proprietors could not be swept away by the British. In the post-1857 period, even in such areas, many merchants encroached on the sectors of traditional dominance by the landlords, but that is, properly speaking, a story of the final consolidation of the semi-feudal modes of exploitation and the further development of their internal contradictions.

Native States as Sanctuaries of Indian Merchants

During the troubled years of the eighteenth century, in various parts of India, great bankers used to lend large sums of money to warring chieftains who included members of the Maratha Confederacy as well as the nawabs and *subedars* who had shared among themselves the remnants of the Mughal empire. The lending by bankers on the guarantee of state finances continued in the native states even in the nineteenth century (British adventurers participated on an enormous scale in the spoliation of the Nawab of Arcot, the Nizam of Hyderabad, and the Nawab of Awadh, but that is yet another story). In 1805, for example, when Colonel Walker, as the agent of the East India Company, was trying to reform the finances of the Gaikwar of Baroda, he 'consolidated the demands of certain shroffs which with interest amounted to Rs. 60,02,861'.[87] This sum did not include the debts owed to the great state bankers of Baroda, Hari Bhakti, and Narsu.

In spite of Colonel Walker's reforms, the Baroda state retained the so-called *potedari* system, under which the state did not maintain any treasury of its own, but instead drew on a handful of state bankers called *potedars* for such sums as it required. 'It did not at any time lodge money with the banker, but it granted him a *varat* or letter of credit on some *izaradar*, or farmer, of the state revenues in one of the *mahals*, who honoured the *varat* at the time of paying in the rent of his farm.'[88] So Sayajirao II entered into a partnership with the *potedars*, often becoming their rivals in lending to his own state. The system of farming revenues to *izaradars* and of using the state banks and the *potedars* as the state treasury continued until Sir T. Madhava Rao was appointed by the British as the Dewan of Baroda.[89] Naturally, under the system, the state bankers possessed enormous funds, some part of which was also employed outside the state. Thus even in 1883, eight years after the reforms of Madhava Rao, the houses of Hari Bhakti and Gopalrao Mairal, the two biggest state bankers of Baroda, were said to possess a capital of seventy-five lakhs of rupees each.[90]

In Hyderabad, Indian bankers acted as treasurers of the Nizam's government until they were virtually supplanted by the firm of William Palmer & Co. which held the whole of the Nizam's territory to ransom. Although determined opposition by Charles Metcalfe, the then Resident at Hyderabad and later, Governor General of India, compelled Palmer & Co. to disgorge some of the gains, the influence of that firm, and later on that of a financier called Dighton, continued.[91] The system of taking loans from the Arabs (who controlled the mercenary forces and became big landlords), the *amils* and the *sahukars* continued. The *sahukars* were often in league with those Europeans who were supposed to have an influence with the Residency and the Nizam's government. In spite of a degree of stabilization achieved by Salar Jang, the most famous minister of the Nizam in the nineteenth century, the Nizam's government continued to borrow money from the *sahukars* as well as from the Bank of Bengal when the latter established a branch there. Thus in 1888, for example, the Nizam's government borrowed money from the following *sahukars* at 6 per cent per annum in lieu of *hundis* on the District Treasuries (as shown in the following table):

Sahukar	Amount of loan (Hallee, sicca Rs.)
Seolal Motilal	5,00,000/-
Bansilal Abirchand	3,25,000/-
Motilal Ramanna Govindass	2,00,000/-

The government proposed to borrow additional amounts in 1889 at 9 per cent per annum from 3 other *sahukars* as 'an exceptional favour'.[92] Bansilal Abirchand was a very big firm which had acted in the 1870s as the Khazanchee of the Bank of Bengal at places as distant as Amritsar and Bombay, and had been a serious contender also for the Khazancheeship in Hyderabad. This access to finances of native states provided many of the *sahukar* firms with the opportunity for investing their funds on a large scale, and correspondingly enabled them to mobilize large amounts of capital when required.[93]

The single most important region which served both as the source and as the base of the biggest mercantile community in India, viz., the Marwaris, was Rajasthan. The petty and not-so-petty principalities of Rajputana served as the organizational basis of various sections of the Marwari traders. Since the *banias* in these states often served as ministers, state treasurers, and tax farmers, they also accumulated some capital from these operations.[94]

The native states provided the merchants also with opportunities for speculation. Not only Hyderabad and Baroda but also a small state such as Jaisalmer, with only a lakh of rupees as revenue in a normal year (around 1908), had its own currency, *Akhai Sahi*, whose value fluctuated widely in relation to the British Indian rupee.[95] Indian merchants played these exchanges, made money, and retained their skills in exchange speculation when the foreign exchange transactions between India and the rest of the world were monopolized by British controlled exchange banks and agency houses.

The native states which provided the initial bases for mercantile firms were not necessarily the major beneficiaries of the industrial ventures launched by these firms. It was Baroda and Gwalior rather than Jaipur and Bikaner which succeeded in attracting mercantile firms promoting industrial ventures. Thus while native states might provide a sustaining medium for Indian mercantile houses, they could not stimulate industrial growth in the absence of several other facilitating conditions.

But that broad statement is true of British Indian territory as well as native states.

A Pre-Bourgeois Law of Inheritance for Preserving Mercantile Wealth

Raja Rammohun Roy, in an essay entitled 'On the right of Hindus over ancestral property',[96] had defended the right of the Bengalis to be governed by the system of law of inheritance, known as Dāyabhāga, rather than by the system knowm as Mitāksharā. Rammohun listed the major points of distinction between the two systems of law, of which the fifth and sixth are worth quoting:

> Fifth. A man having a share of undivided real property is not authorized to make a sale or gift of it without the consent of the rest of his partners according to the Mitāksharā but according to the Dāyabhāga he can dispose of it at his own free will.
>
> Sixth. A man in possession of ancestral real property, though not under any tenure limiting it to the successive generations of his family, is not authorized to dispose of it, by sale or gift, without the consent of his sons and grandsons, according to the Mitāksharā, while according to the Dāyabhāga, he has the power to alienate his property at his own free will.

According to Rammohun, under the Dāyabhāga dispensation, 'Anyone possessed of landed property, whether self-acquired or ancestral, has been able, under the long-established law of the land, to procure easily, on the credit of that property, loans of money to lay out on the improvement of his estate, in trade or manufactures, whereby he enriches himself and his family and benefits the country.'[97] Rammohun protested against a reported proposal to replace the Dāyabhāga with the Mitāksharā system, which governed the Hindus in practically the whole of India outside Bengal. He also protested against the upsetting of the long-established precedent that a father could not only dispose of any self-acquired property but also of ancestral property without the consent of his sons or grandsons (even though it might be shown that this precedent was due to Raghunandana, rather than to Jimutavāhana, the author of the Dāyabhāga principles).

A standard text on Hindu law puts the essential distinction between the Dāyabhāga and the Mitāksharā systems as follows:

> The Mitāksharā recognizes two modes of devolution of property, namely, survivorship and succession. The rule of survivorship

applies to joint family property; the rules of succession apply to property held in absolute severalty by the last owner.

The Dāyabhāga recognizes only one mode of devolution, namely, succession. It does not recognize the rule of survivorship even in the case of joint family property. The reason is that while every member of a Mitāksharā joint family has only an *undivided* interest in the joint property, a member of a Dāyabhāga joint family holds his share in *quasi-severalty*, so that it passes on his death to his heirs as if he was absolutely seized thereof, and not to the surviving coparceners as under the Mitāksharā law.[98]

The Dāyabhāga is a far more individualistic system of law than the Mitāksharā, and the notion of private property embodied in the discourse of Jimutavāhana fits the requirement of mobility of capital demanded by a full-fledged capitalist economy far better than the Mitāksharā does. Ironically enough, however, as with many other principles upheld by the leaders of the Anglophile Bengali intelligentsia of the nineteenth century, the Dāyabhāga system proved quite subversive of the foundations of Indian property in Bengal. The undisputed disposers of property were quickly separated from their patrimony as they became embroiled in insolvency suits as partners of defaulting (and often decamping) Europeans, and designing creditors found it easy to mulct young heirs when their propensity to squander their inherited wealth could not be curbed by family authority. In contrast, those whose property was held jointly with other coparceners found it easier to protect it because of the legal uncertainty involved. The Hindu joint family system of property holding also aided tax avoidance and evasion in the post-independence period, but that belongs to a different phase of the history of the Indian mercantile community. Along with the relative invulnerability of the jointly held mercantile properties, the uncodified and customary nature of Hindu law made the seizure of debtors' property rather difficult, particularly within the jurisdiction of native states. The Mitākshārā system was appropriate to the legal facade for the continuation of the familial basis of the Indian merchants' business.

The Survival Value of Intergroup and Intragroup Cohesion among Merchants

The merchants of colonial India inherited an India-wide network of commercial and financial relations. The *hundis* of great bankers were honoured throughout most of India;[99] insurance was available for commodities and bullion transported from one region of the country to others, and the rates of insurance were remarkably low. As late as 1873, the Bank of Bengal agent at Hyderabad was instructed to send specie via shroffs' insurance, rather than by any other means of remittance. There were *jakhmi hundis* which combined the characteristics of an insurance policy and an exchange bill. Although deposit banking had not developed on a systematic basis all over the country, there were many bankers who received deposits.

We have seen earlier that there were many commercial associations and civic organizations which cut across caste and community lines. Some of these organizations survived into colonial times. However, the British rulers, unlike their predecessors, gave only a token recognition or none at all, to *Nagarseths*, leaders of *mahajan panchayats*, or *chaudharis* of market places.[100]

However, in spite of official indifference or hostility, many of the inter-caste and intercommunity links among mercantile communities in British India survived.[101] And most of the important pre-British mercantile communities of the interior survived as well.

For the early part of the nineteenth century, we have numerous accounts of the high level of inter-regional organization maintained by the Indian mercantile communities as well as by individual business houses. For example, James Douglas gave a list of twenty-one 'conspicuous' shroffs established in Bombay in 1845, some of whom, such as Jivraj Balloo, were established before the nineteenth century opened.[102] According to him, 'you might have gone to almost any of them, and if you wished a draft on any place from Peshawar to Travancore, you would get it.' Some of the most remarkable examples of the resistance of mercantile communities against the ill effects of colonial rule relate to their ability, in particular areas and particular periods, to overcome the monetary stringency caused by the continuous drain of silver from India. Thus in Gujarat, the merchants used *ant* (the fictitious currency for settling accounts without the actual transfer of coin) extensively when the British temporarily closed the mint and when British policies caused a shortage of medium of exchange. This system persisted till 1846 at Dhollera for settling all mercantile transactions, and at least up to the end of the 1870s at Ahmedabad for carrying out all banking transactions.[103] This may have partly insulated Gujarati merchants against the long depression which affected most parts of India between 1826–7 and 1852–3 or so. At Mirzapur and nearby towns, the system grew up of using *toras* of Farruckabad coins, bearing the names and guarantees of important merchants, as the medium of exchange. The Farruckabad rupees had a lower bullion value than the British Indian rupee, but the *toras* might even circulate at a premium from time to time. The pressure to invest the money and thereby keep the *toras* in circulation kept interest rates low at Mirzapur—sometimes they were lower than in Calcutta or London.[104]

Coming to particular communities, Colonel Wade reported for the 1830s that the only people who dealt regularly in European commodities in the 'countries beyond the Indus and Sutlej' were the *banias* of Jodhpur and Shekhawati. In order to illustrate the scale of Marwari connections, he gave the example of ten sons and grandson of Bugotee Ram, who was the Treasurer or *Photedar* of the then Nawab of Fatehpur. These ten descendants of Bugotee Ram, who were themselves called *Photedars* (or Poddars), had *gomostahs* or agents at the following places (besides their houses at Ramgarh in Shekhavati and Choroo in Bikaner): Bombay, Surat, Baonajar, Muscat, Pali, Jodhpur, Nagore, Jaisalmir, Shikarpur, Ajmir, Bikaner, Jullundur, Amritsar, Lahore, Kashmir, Ludhiana, Patiala, Nabha, Jagadre, Hissar, Hase, Bewanee, Rohtak, Delhi, Jaipur, Kotah, Amraoti, Ujjain, Indore, Nagpur, Hyderabad, Poona, Hathras, Chandausi, Farruckabad, Mathura, Agra, Mirzapur, Benares, Murshidabad, Patna, Calcutta, and Goalpara. The *gomostahs* were all from Bikaner or Shekhavati.[105]

Colonel Wade stressed the economies enjoyed by a house with such far-ranging connections:

> They are able to carry on trade with smaller profits and this combined with their extensive connections and the good understanding they have with one another, has given them a decided commercial ascendancy in upper India. They are the general insurers for other people, but the superior facilities they enjoy and the extensive nature of their transactions render insurance unnecessary in their own case.

While the Marwaris became the biggest single business community of modern India, Bānjārās, originating from the same region, either became cultivators or were reduced to the status of scheduled tribes or gypsies. The story of the dramatic rise and fall of the Bānjārās is indicative of the changes brought about by the consolidation of British paramountcy.

The Chārans or Bhāts of Rajasthan were supposed to be the ancestors of Banjārās. Their sacred character gave them protection in their native lands, and they turned to the business of carrying messages and goods.[106] In the late seventeenth and eighteenth centuries they emerged as the suppliers of goods to the warring Mughal and other armies as well as to the civilian population of practically the whole region from Punjab to Mysore, and from Maharashtra to Bihar. As more and more of the subcontinent passed under British sway, and as the new rulers organized their own system of army supplies, the importance of Bānjārās as army suppliers declined. As armed bands, they also came into conflict with local rulers and the general populace in many regions. They were to be found as carriers of goods in the Central Provinces and Hyderabad even as late as the 1860s.[107] The decline of the Bānjārās as merchants was completed by their inability to establish any permanent trading stations. In parts of Uttar Pradesh, they took to the profession of breeding and dealing in cattle or horses.[108] In other areas they were described as dacoits (they took an important part in the Great Indian Revolt of 1857).[109] In many parts of the country, they became pedlars, leading a life very similar to that of the gypsies. The failure of the Bānjārās to adapt to the new conditions where the services earlier performed by them became obsolete, their failure to obtain a lien on any usufruct of the land, and some weakness in their internal organization which is still to be cleared up by intensive research seem to have conspired together to reduce them to the status of scheduled tribes in parts of India. The Gosain traders in this respect provide a partial contrast. The Dasnami Gosains resembled the Bānjārās in many ways. They became traders and financiers on a large scale in the eighteenth century. But their *maths* served as permanent stations for them, and although their trade declined, in some areas such as Benares and Tarakeshwar in Bengal, they seem to have accumulated a considerable amount of property.[110]

Another community which illustrates some of the problems of determining the precise reasons for rise and fall of particular groups as merchants is that of the Lohānās of Punjab,

Sind, and northern Gujarat. The Lohānās of Cutch apparently owed their pre-eminence in the seventeenth century to royal favour. In the eighteenth century, they were persecuted by the local rulers and declined in importance. By 1880, the Gazetteer for Cutch reported that few of them were men of much wealth and position within the limits of Cutch.[111] In their most important base, Shikarpur, they were still an important trading community, although the Imperial Gazetteer considered it necessary to differentiate between *Amils* and other Lohānās, and classed the *Amils* as clerks and government servants as well as traders.[112] The *Amils* emerged as important financiers in Hyderabad and Multani shroffs were to be found all over India, but many of them were Marwaris rather than Lohānās. The general drying up of opportunities for trade and finance in Sind with the incursion of Europeans into transfrontier trade seems to have taken a toll on many of the Lohānās in their mercantile role.[113]

In the case of Lohānās it was more the imperfect adjustment to rapidly changing opportunities for trade and finance than any lack of internal cohesion that seems to have accounted for their relative retardation as a mercantile community (compared with the Bhatias or the Marwaris). All successful mercantile communities seem to have been marked by a high degree of formalization of the rules of training, recruitment, and general intra-community relations. This can be seen in the case of the Komatis or Chettiars of the south as well as the Marwaris and the Gujarati *banias*.

The Gujarati *banias* and the Komatis both possessed elaborate arithmetical tables with fractions and multiples of rupees and annas, which both sharpened the powers of quick calculation required of a trader or banker and facilitated the keeping of accounts. Both the communities seem also to have possessed a special language including a set of signs for striking bargains among themselves.[114] (A special set of signs or sounds for bargaining and keeping trade secrets seems to have been characteristic of many other closely knit trading groups.) The training of young merchants generally took place within the mercantile establishment itself. As late as 1909, most Nattukottai Chettis apparently regarded English education as rather unpractical, preferring the long apprenticeship to which young Chettis were subjected traditionally.[115]

The Marwari traders generally operated within a well-regulated community framework, any newcomer to a region finding help from his caste fellows, or from other traders from the same region. The Marwari settlers in a group of villages generally chose some leading men to form a council or *panchayat*, for arbitrating in 'social disputes, arranging for the support of their temple and its worship, and for the management of the provident fund....'[116] Similarly, the Komatis settled in each place had a leader called a Podda Setti, and the Kalinga Komatis in addition had a headman styled Kularaja or Vaisyaraje, for several villages. It was these leaders who settled important questions relating to the caste, by fine, excommunication, etc. 'Komatis (had) recourse to the established courts of justice only as a last resort. They (were) consulted by other castes in the settlement of their disputes....'[117]

The Nattukottai Chettiars from the Ramnad district of Madras had an elaborate system of training and recruitment of members of the community. A boy of ten or twelve was expected to apply himself to business, learn accounts, and attend the shop of his father. After his marriage, all his expenses were debited to him, and he was expected to save as much as he could out of the allowance or initial capital granted to him. Every rupee earned was laid out at as high a rate of interest as possible.[118]

The Chettiars travelled far outside their district to all parts of south India and set up as traders and moneylenders in Sri Lanka, Malaysia, Burma, Indo-China, and Indonesia. There was an elaborate system of recruitment of agents (belonging to the same community as the owners of the home firm) for these places, which was described thus in 1907:

> People of moderate means usually elect to go to distant places as agents of the different firms that have their head offices either at Madura or in the *zamindars* of Ramnad and Sivaganga. The pay of a local agent varies directly with the distance of the place to which he is posted. If he is kept at Madura, he gets Rs. 100 per mensem; if sent to Burma, he gets three times as much, and, if to Natal, about twice the latter sum. If an agent proves himself to be an industrious and energetic man, he is usually given a percentage on the profits. The tenure of office is for three years, six months before the expiry of which the next agent is sent over to work conjointly with the existing one, and study the local conditions. On relief,

the agent returns directly to his head office, and delivers over his papers, and then goes on to his own village. With this, his connection with his firm practically ceases. He enjoys his well earned rest of three years, at the end of which he seeks re-employment either under his old firm, or under any other. The former he is bound to do, if he has taken a percentage on the profits during his previous tenure of office. If the old firm rejects him when he so offers himself, then he is at liberty to enter service under others.[119]

The Nattukottai Chettis were permitted by custom to partition the property among the brothers but voluntarily decided to adopt a joint family system for purposes of management, although individual members were encouraged to keep a part under their own control for purposes of business.[120]

This organizational pattern was a sophisticated combination of pursuit of individual profit and control and risk-sharing through a community code of mutual trust and confidence, and made abundant sense in a world of uncertainty.[121] Many outside this community such as poor peasants and a sizeable section within the community, viz., the women, bore the brunt of this system of community risk-sharing and individual profit-maximizing, but that is a matter we cannot pursue here. While the family was the basic unit of control in the business organizations of the Chettiars, the Marwaris or the Gujarati *banias*, the employment of members of other castes as important links in the organizational set-up was not unknown. For example, the Meshri *banias* sometimes employed Brahmans (and Parsis) as clerks and managers;[122] and some Marwari firms also employed Brahmans as clerks.[123] But employment of men from the same caste or community was more common.

While Indian industrialists are generally accused of being rather unadventurous, Indian merchants were often accused of a great fondness for speculation. The role of speculation in rationalizing capitalist activities in general is as yet unexplored. But there seems to be evidence that certain forms of speculation or gambling were institutionalized among Gujarati *banias* as well as the Marwaris. In Ahmedabad, for example, time bargains or forward trading in *ant* was widely prevalent,[124] and time bargains (called *vaida*) in opium and other commercially important commodities 'except perhaps grain' were rife in 1849 as well as 1879.[125] Time bargains in shares proved to be one of the most important forces feeding speculation in Bombay in the period 1864–6, and bringing down the Bank of Bombay and many other financial institutions and real estate companies. The custom of gambling seems to have been built into the religious ritual of *banias* of Gujarat and Central Provinces. In both the regions, Divali was an extremely important festival for the *banias*, and apparently continues to be so. The *banias* close their accounts on this day.

> *Divali-baki* or loans outstanding on Divali are not liked by merchants who try their best to repay their loans and recover their bills in the days preceding *Divali*.... Merchants transact business of new varieties of goods and give some cash to one another to enter the account of sale and purchase in the new books as a token of goodwill. They also send some items of their merchandise to their permanent customers as *boni* or the auspicious first deal and enter their names in the new books.[126]

Describing very similar customs as prevailing among the *banias* of Central Provinces, Russell and Hira Lal added: 'The *Banias* and Hindus generally think it requisite to gamble at *Divali* in order to bring good luck during the coming year; all classes indulge in a little speculation in this season.'[127]

The Indore state derived a regular income from *satta* (or forward exchange combined with gambling) transactions in opium.[128] Thus a state run on pre-capitalist principles could accommodate a system which the British administrators often regarded as anathema. Successful merchants seem to have regarded it essential for maintaining their profession that they should have their speculative activities to counter or take advantage of the instability caused by harvest fluctuations.

Epilogue

A detailed account of the way in which successful mercantile groups collaborated with or dissociated themselves from the European-dominated export–import transactions or European-style financial and industrial firms is a separate theme and we shall not pursue it in this paper. Most of the successful merchants in most of the regions collaborated with the British both commercially and politically.[129] During the Great Indian Revolt of 1857, merchants and moneylenders were often subjects of attack by the revolting Indians, and merchants generally collaborated with the British.[130]

However, there were exceptions, although they were few in number. For example, Ramji Dass, of the Gurwala banking firm of Delhi, lent large sums to Emperor Bahadur Shah II during 1857–8 and was hanged by the British for his sins.[131] More typical was the case of Chunnamal Salig Ram, who had made a fortune out of supplying shawls, brocades, and piecegoods to the Emperor's *toshakhana* but simply deserted his cause and lay low until the storm blew over, to wax prosperous again under British rule. Yet a third pattern was provided by Budri Dass, the great grandfather of Lala Shri Ram, who amassed a fortune as the treasurer of the British cantonment at Karnal, as *kotwal* at the British cantonments of Ferozpore and Delhi, and as a loyal collaborator of the British during the Revolt of 1857.[132]

However, the degree or pattern of collaboration or involvement of Indian traders and financiers with European merchants was by no means constant over time. Many Parsi merchants achieved a degree of autonomy vis-a-vis foreign merchants over the course of the nineteenth century. Many Marwaris who had kept a distance between the Europeans and themselves became collaborators of British firms. In the twentieth century, the mutual relations between foreign capital and different mercantile groups changed again.

Moreover, at the lower levels, among *baladia* (cattle-owning) travelling merchants or smaller traders, there are numerous examples of resistance against British rule. An intelligible account of the variations in merchants' behaviour must take into account both the political and economic constraints on their freedom of action and relate the evolution of such constraints to the larger movements of Indian society. A beginning in this direction is yet to be made at least as far as the analysis of mercantile behaviour in the nineteenth century is concerned.

Acknowledgement

An earlier version of the paper was presented at the seminar on Aspects of the Indian Economy, Society and Politics in Modern India organized by the Nehru Memorial Museum and Library, New Delhi, between 15 and 18 December 1980. I am indebted to the participants in that seminar for many illuminating comments. Sabyasachi Bhattacharya, Nirmal Chandra,

Partha Chatterjee, Amalendu Guha, Saugata Mukherjee, Abhik Ray, Indrani Ray, and Sumit Sarkar helped with comments and suggestions. I owe a special debt of gratitude to Gautam Bhadra and Gyan Pandey for extremely useful comments and further references. None of the persons mentioned are responsible for any remaining errors.

Notes and References

1. Published by Progress Publishers, Moscow, 1966; Chapter XX, 'Historical Facts about Merchant's Capital'.
2. Karl Marx, *Theories of Surplus Value*, part III (Moscow: Progress Publishers, 1971), pp. 288–9.
3. Published by Institute of Pacific Relations, New York, 1959; M.V. Namjoshi assisted Gadgil in writing this book.
4. Published by People's Publishing House, New Delhi, 1964.
5. Irfan Habib in his authoritative article 'Potentialities of Capitalistic Development in the Economy of Mughal India', *Enquiry*, Winter 1971, gives a lucid account of the dominant mode of appropriation under the Mughal dispensation and of the importance of merchant capital in Mughal India. But he

does not draw the inference that the mode of appropriation that thwarted the expansion of the agrarian economy through real capital formation and technical change also paradoxically strengthened merchant capital. He also attaches too much importance to the alleged dislocations of the eighteenth century in curbing the growth of incipient capitalistic modes of organization of production.

6. There are two other books by Soviet scholars, namely, A.I. Chicherov's *India: Economic Development in the 16th–18th Centuries: Outline History of Crafts and Trade* (Moscow: Nauka Publishing House, 1971) and A.I. Levkovsky's *Capitalism in India: Basic Trends in Its Development* (New Delhi: People's Publishing House, 1972). Although quite useful for discussion of particular issues, Chicherov's book suffers from a rather mechanical view of the evolution of socio-economic formations in India, and Levkovsky's from an uncritical attitude towards the data he gathers from a variety of sources. In any case, neither of the books is primarily focused on the functioning or organization of business groups.

7. This aspect is referred to by Pavlov in *The Indian Capitalist Class*, Chapter 2.

8. See J.C. Van Leur, *Indonesian Trade and Society* (The Hague: W. Van Hoeva, 1955). Van Leur's views have been reiterated by Niels

Steenagaard and criticized, among others, by K.N. Chaudhuri and Ashin Dasgupta. It may be worth pointing out that van Leur's distinction did not have much validity in the city states of Renaissance Italy either. See G. Luzzata, 'Small and Great Merchants in the Italian Cities of the Renaissance', in *Enterprise and Secular Change* edited by F.C. Lane and J.C. Riemersma (London: Allen and Unwin, 1953). The enormous fluctuations in commodity prices dictated a high degree of diversification as a hedging device; and the uncertainty of political fortunes and connected with that the uncertainty of fortunes of even big merchants dictated that a high proportion of resources should be kept regionally liquid. The latter demanded pyramidal structure of control and resort to petty trade and moneylending in the local context.

9. See, for example, his statement in section 5 of *Origins of the Modern Indian Business Class*: 'Accumulation of capital, innovation, etc. were much more possible and were likely to be more evidenced among the trading and financing classes than among the large number of scattered tradition-bound and relatively poor artisans.' There is no evidence that the traders and financiers were any less tradition-bound than artisans in India or that they pioneered any more innovations than

these artisans. They definitely accumulated more capital, but that capital was mostly used to perpetuate a mode of exploitation and control which severely inhibited innovations in production methods.

10. For an example, see Ali Muhammad Khan, *Mirat-i-Ahmadi*, translated by M.F. Lokhandwalla (Baroda: Oriental Institute, 1965), chapter 156.

11. For examples, see A. Das Gupta, 'The Merchants of Surat, c. 1700–50', in *Elites in South Asia* edited by E. Leach and S.N. Mukherjee (Cambridge: Cambridge University Press, 1970) and M.J. Mehta, 'Business Environment, Urbanization and Economic Change in India: A Case Study of Ahmedabad in the 19th Century', *Vidya* (The Journal of Gujarat University), January 1981, and references cited there.

12. D.R. Gadgil, *Origins of the Modern Indian Business Class*, section 7; M.N. Pearson, 'Political Participation in Mughal India', *The Indian Economic and Social History Review* (later abbreviated as *IESHR*), IX (4), December 1972; Gautam Bhadra, 'Social Groups and Social Relations in the Town of Murshidabad', *Indian Historical Review*, II (2); and C. A. Bayly, 'Indian Merchants in a "Traditional" Setting: Benares, 1780–1830', in *The Imperial Impact: Studies in the Economic History of Africa and India* edited by C. Dewey and A.G. Hopkins (London: The Athlone Press, 1978).

13. J. Tod, *Annals and Antiquities of Rajasthan* (first published, 1829; reprinted in New Delhi: N.B.D. Publishers, 1978, vol. I), pp. 119–20, 553.

14. *Pykars* were native agents, a class of brokers responsible for providing silk good to the English East India Company in Bengal. They made advances to cultivators of mulberry and rearers of silk worms.

15. On the role of the Armenians in Indian and Asian trade, see M.J. Seth, *Armenians in India* (Calcutta, 1937), chapters 21–34; R.W. Ferrier, 'The Armenians and the East India Company in Persia in the Seventeenth and Early Eighteenth Centuries', *Economic History Review*, second series, XXVI, 1973; S. Chaudhuri, *Trade and Commercial Organization in Bengal* (Calcutta: Firma K.L. Mukhopadhyaya, 1975). On the importance of petty traders in the economy of Mughal India, see Gautam Bhadra, 'Mogul Jugey Bharatiya Banik' (in Bengali), *Ekshan, Sharadiya* (Autumn), B.S. 1387 (1980 A.D.).

16. For the description of the activities of the house of Jagat Seth in relation to the *subedars* and nawabs of Bengal, see J.H. Little, *The House of Jagatseth*, with an introduction by N.K. Sinha (Calcutta: Calcutta Historical Society, 1967).

17. For a summary of the evidence relating to such activities, see Pavlov, *The Indian Capitalist Class*, chapter 2.

18. See M.N. Pearson, 'Indigenous Dominance in a Colonial Economy: The Goa Rendas,

1600–1670', *Mare Luso-Indicum*, Tome II, 1972, published for Centre de recherches de l'histoire et de la philology de la IVe section de l'École pratique des hautes études, by Librairie Droz, Geneva, 1973. Port dues at Surat or customs duties (on salt) at the inland mart of Palli (in Rajasthan) could amount to a substantial fraction of total state revenues.

19. Abdul Karim, *Dacca: The Mughal Capital* (Dacca: Asiatic Society, 1964), p. 16.

20. Mir Jumla was a powerful general of Emperor Aurangzeb. The emperor was fearful of Mir Jumla's ambitions and made him the governor of Bengal, a distant province.

21. There were specific instructions against indiscriminate sequestration. See, for example, Ali Muhammad Khan, *Mirat-i-Ahmadi*, chapter 109 ('A Copy of a Memorandum of Court Events in Respect of Confiscation of Mansabdars' property').

22. See, for some examples of the vicissitudes of fortune of Muslim merchant princes, the cases of Mulla Muhammad Ali and Ahmed Challeby, in Ali Muhammad Khan, *Mirat-i-Ahmadi*, chapters 208, 216, and 219. Hindu merchants also suffered because of personal quarrels with rulers or other merchants who had the ear of the rulers, but their families often survived as members of the 'peaceable' communities.

23. For Rajasthan, see Dilbagh Singh, 'The Role of the Mahajans in the Rural Economy in Eastern Rajasthan during the 18th Century', paper presented at the Indian History Congress, Chandigarh, 1973.

24. See Hitesranjan Sanyal, 'Social Mobility in Bengal: Its Sources and Constraints', *Indian Historical Review*, II (1), July 1975, esp. pp. 87–8.

25. Tod, *Annals and Antiquities of Rajasthan*, vol. I, pp. 554–6.

26. See in this connection, Bhadra, 'Mogul Jugey Bharatiya Banik', pp. 75–6.

27. For some examples, see Ashin Das Gupta, *Indian Merchants and the Decline of Surat: c.1700–1750* (Wiesbaden: Franz Steiner Verlag, 1979), pp. 36–42.

28. See Gadgil, *Origins of the Modern Indian Business Class*, sections 6–10, and Habib, 'Potentialities of Capitalistic Development in the Economy of Mughal India', section 3. Habib seems to overestimate the importance of the royal *kārkhānās* as potentially capitalistic organizations. In a situation in which the wages of artisans were extremely low, and owners of capital had little incentive to economize on labour by organizing large-scale production, royal *kārkhānās* could hardly lead to a systematic development of large-scale production or production techniques.

29. On Portuguese conquests and operations in the Arabian Sea, Bay of Bengal, and the Indian Ocean, see C.R. Boxer, *The Portuguese Seaborne Empire 1415–1825* (Harmondsworth, Middlesex: Penguin Books, 1973), chapter 2, and on Gujarati merchants' adaptation to the Portuguese presence, see M.N. Pearson, *Merchants and Rulers in Gujarat: The Response to the Portuguese in the Sixteenth Century* (Berkeley: University of California Press, 1976), chapter 4.

30. Om Prakash, 'The European Trading Companies and the Merchants of Bengal, 1650–1725', *IESHR*, I (3), January–March 1964.

31. K.N. Chaudhuri, *The Trading World of Asia and the English East India Company: 1660–1760* (Cambridge: Cambridge University Press, 1978), chapter 6, and I. Bruce Watson, 'Fortifications and the "Idia" of Force in Early East India Company Relations with India', *Past and Present*, LXXXVIII, August 1980.

32. K.N. Chaudhuri, *The Trading World of Asia*, pp. 508–10.

33. This is the crux of the problem of trade between 'unequal partners' that was pointed out by me in my critique of K.N. Chaudhuri in 'Towards an "Inter-continental Model": Some Trends in Indo-European Trade in the Seventeenth century', *IESHR*, VI (1), March 1969. See A.K.

Bagchi, 'Comments on "Some Trends in India's Foreign Trade in the Seventeenth Century"', *IESHR*, March 1969.

34. Thus, many traders dealing with the house of Jagatseth were supposed to have been ruined in the process. See N.K. Sinha's 'Introduction' to Little, *House of Jagatseth*.

35. See, for examples of resistance by Indian merchants to the systematic attempt at the exercise of monopoly control by the English East India Company in the period 1670–1720, and ruin of some of the big Indian merchants in the process, S. Chaudhuri, *Trade and Commercial Organization in Bengal*, chapter 4. The way the historian's language is influenced by the kind of source material he uses (East India Company's records in this case) is illustrated by this chapter. Indian merchants are seen as trying to organize 'rings' or dealing with 'interlopers', whereas the constant attempt of the English Company to exercise monopoly control is played down.

36. See K.N. Chaudhuri, *Trading World of Asia*, chapter 12; and S. Chaudhuri, *Trade and Commercial Organization in Bengal*, chapters 4 and 5. See also my review of K.N. Chaudhuri's *Trading World of Asia* in the *Times of India*, 2 September 1979. Indrani Ray in her 'Multiple Faces of the Early 18th Century Indian Merchants', Occasional Paper no. 29

(August 1980), Center for Studies in Social Sciences, Calcutta, has elaborated on the theme of subordination of Indian collaborators by various European trading companies.

37. Marx, *Capital*, vol. III, p. 325.

38. F. Buchanan, *A Journey from Madras through the Countries of Mysore, Canara and Malabar*, vol. I–III (London, 1807).

39. See S.K. Sen (ed.), *Edmund Burke on Indian Economy* (Calcutta: Progressive Publishers, 1969). The usefulness of this edition is impaired by unexplained excisions and lack of the full apparatus of citation.

40. B.C. Barui, *The Salt Industry of Bengal: The Relations of Production in the Industry and Trade in Salt 1757–1800* (thesis submitted for the degree of PhD (Arts) of the Calcutta University, 1979), chapter 2.

41. The following account is based on G. Bhadra, *The Role of Pykars in the Silk Industry of Bengal (c.1765–1830)* (typescript).

42. See N.K. Sinha, *The Economic History of Bengal*, vol. I (Calcutta: Firma K.L. Mukhopadhyay, 1965), chapters 2–4 and 9, and Debendra Bijoy Mitra, *The Cotton Weavers of Bengal 1757–1833* (Calcutta: Firma K.L.M., 1978).

43. On the continued sale of coarse goods outside the controlling authority of the Company, see N.K. Sinha, *The Economic History of*

Bengal 1793–1848, vol. III (Calcutta: Firma K.L. Mukhopadhyay, 1970), p. 10.

44. B.C. Barui, 'The Smuggling Trade of Opium in the Bengal Presidency: 1793–1817', *Bengal Past and Present*, July–December 1975; and Barui, 'The Salt Industry of Bengal', chapters 5 and 6.

45. On the details of the revenue settlements made by the Company, see N.K. Sinha, *The Economic History of Bengal*, vol. II (Calcutta: Firma, K.L. Mukhopadhyay, 1968): N.K. Sinha, *The Economic History of Bengal*, vol. III; Sirajul Islam, *The Permanent Settlement in Bengal: A Study of Its Operation 1790–1819* (Dacca: Bangla Academy, 1979), chapters 1–3; and Ratnalekha Ray, *Change in Bengal Agrarian Society* (New Delhi: Manohar, 1979), chapters 2 and 4.

46. N.K. Sinha, *The Economic History of Bengal*, vol. I, pp. 169–70.

47. N.K. Sinha, *The Economic History of Bengal*, vol. I, p. 168–9.

48. Bhadra, *The Role of Pykars in the Silk Industry of Bengal*, section 6.

49. See Gyan Pandey, *Economic Dislocation in Nineteenth-Century Eastern U.P. Some Implications of the Decline of Artisanal Industry in Colonial India*, Occasional Paper no. 37, Centre for Studies in Social Sciences, Calcutta, May 1981, p. 33.

50. On the use of the term *banian* or *banyan*, see H. Yule and A.C. Burnell, *Hobson-Jobson*, new edition by W. Crooke (reprinted in New Delhi: Munshiram Manoharlal, 1968), pp. 63–4.

51. See Blair B. Kling, *Partner in Empire* (Berkeley: University of California Press, 1976), p. 19.

52. N.K. Sinha, *Economic History of Bengal*, vol. I, pp. 104–6, vol. II, p. 223; and Islam, *The Permanent Settlement in Bengal*, p. 20.

53. See Kling, *Partner in Empire*, chapter 10.

54. See A.K. Bagchi, *Private Investment in India 1900–1939* (London: Cambridge University Press, 1972), chapter 6 and A.K. Bagchi, 'Reflections on Patterns of Regional Growth in India under British rule', *Bengal Past and Present*, January–June 1976.

55. N. Benjamin, 'Raw Cotton of Western India—A Comment', *IESHR*, X (1), 1973.

56. For the general background of trade and exchange in Bombay in the nineteenth century, see J. Douglas, *Glimpses of Bombay and Western India* (London, 1900); R.J.F. Sullivan, *One Hundred Years of Bombay: History of the Bombay Chamber of Commerce 1836–1936* (Bombay: Times of India Press, 1937); P. Nightingale, *Trade and Empire in Western India 1784–1806* (Cambridge: Cambridge University Press, 1970); A. Guha, 'Raw Cotton of Western India: Output, Transportation and Marketing',

IESHR, IX (1), 1972; and C. Dobbin, *Urban Leadership in Western India* (London: Oxford University Press, 1972), chapter 1.

57. The prospectus for the Anglo-Indian Spinning and Manufacturing Company, floated in Manchester 1874 for operating in Bombay, estimated that Indian mill-made cotton goods consumed in India enjoyed a cost advantage of 30 per cent compared with similar goods exported from England to India. It quoted one Lancashire man managing a mill in India as saying that an efficiently managed mill there ought to return its cost in three years. The appeal to prospective shareholders in India on behalf of the mill (one-third of the shares were reserved for subscription in India) quoted the following figures of the latest dividend rates declared by Bombay mills (figures in per cent):

Alliance	32	Great Eastern	24
Bombay Royal	19	Alexandra	24
Manockjee Petit	15	Albert	20
Oriental	30	Morarjee Goculdass	20
Bombay United	20	Jivraj Baloo	23

These attractive figures were well below the *profit* rates realized by the pioneer cotton mills.

58. See A.C. Lyall, *Gazetteer for the Hyderabad Assigned Districts Commonly Called Berar* (Bombay, 1870), chapter 12.

59. Gazetteer of the Bombay Presidency, vol. II, *Surat and Broach* (Bombay: Government Central Press, 1877), p. 446.

60. Gazetteer of the Bombay Presidency, vol. XII, *Khandesh* (Bombay: Government Central Press, 1880), chapter 5, esp. pp. 191–3.

61. See M. Vicziany, 'Bombay Merchants and Structural Changes in the Export Community 1850 to 1880', in *Economy and Society: Essays in Indian Economic and Social History* edited by K.N. Chaudhuri and C.J. Dewey (Delhi: Oxford University Press, 1979). The degree of decline of Indian share in cotton exports has been probably overestimated in this paper, for according to some contemporary evidence, a considerable amount of Indian-owned cotton was exported under the umbrella of European names; cf also footnote 53.

62. The literature on the Bengali *babu* culture is enormous. A reference to the anthologies compiled by Brajendranath Bandyopadhyay and Benoy Ghose and to their own books will provide enough documentation. The Parsi craze for imitating the lifestyles of the British is well known. In 1834, the Governor of Bombay issued a minute directing that the following persons should be addressed as 'Esquire':

Juggonath Sunkersett, Bomanjee Hormusjee, Framjee Cowasjee, Nowrojee Jamsetjee, Jamsetjee Jejeebhoy, Dadabhai Pestonjee, Dhakjee Dadajee, Cursetjee Cowasjee, Cursetjee Cowasjee Dady, Mohamad Ali Rogay, Cursetjee Rustomjee, Mohamed Ibrahim Mocha, Hormasjee Bhicajee Chinoy. See J.M. Maclean, *A Guide to Bombay*, fifth edition (Bombay, 1880), p. 37. Of the thirteen honorary squires, at least nine were Parsis. This was a much higher proportion than that of Parsis to the Indian population of the Bombay city or of the number of Parsi merchants to the total number of Indians in the city. It is also interesting that the only baronets to be created by the British from their Indian or Asian subjects in India in the nineteenth century seem to have been three Parsis (Jamsetjee Jejeebhoy, Cowasjee Jehangir, and Dinshaw Manokjee Petit) and one Baghdadi Jew settled in Bombay (Albert David Sassoon).

63. See Kling, *Partner in Empire*, chapters 1, 2 and 7; and R.A. Wadia, *The Bombay Dockyard and the Wadia Master-Builders* (Bombay, 1957), chapter 18.

64. For a description of Tipu's policies in regard to trade, see M.H. Gopal, *Tipu Sultan's Mysore* (Bombay: Popular Prakashan, 1971), chapter 2.

65. Buchanan, *Journey from Madras*, vol. II, p. 33.

66. Buchanan, *Journey from Madras*, vol. II, pp. 239–40.

67. Buchanan, *Journey from Madras*, vol. II, p. 264.

68. Gopal, *Tipu Sultan's Mysore*, pp. 15–16.

69. C.K. Kareem, *Kerala under Haidar Ali and Tipu Sultan* (Ernakulam: Paico Publishing House, 1973), p. 168.

70. Gazetteer of the Bombay Presidency, vol. IX, part I, *Gujarat Population: Hindus* (Bombay: Government Central Press, 1901), p. 178.

71. For an earlier discussion on similar lines of the obstacles against craftsmen becoming industrial capitalists in British India, see D.H. Buchanan, *The Development of Capitalistic Enterprise in India* (first published, 1934; reprinted in London: Frank Cass, 1966), pp. 145–6, and 343. Buchanan distinguished between the 'putting-out' system and 'the finance and order' system, which according to him, characterized the relationship of the artisan and the merchant. Under the latter system, the producer continues to superintend the work and the merchant can exploit the labour of the whole family of the craftsman. See Buchanan, *The Development of Capitalistic Enterprise in India*, pp. 110–11. However, by the beginning of the twentieth century, in many parts of India, employers were putting several workers together under one shed for producing silk and cotton cloth. Furthermore,

under the putting-out system also the labour of the whole family was often at the disposal of the putter-out.

72. Cf. Bagchi, 'Reflections on Patterns of Regional Growth', p. 264.

73. See A.E. Musson, 'Editor's Introduction' and 'The Diffusion of Technology in Great Britain during the Industrial Revolution', in *Science Technology and Economic Growth in the Nineteenth Century* edited by A.E. Musson (London: Methuen, 1972).

74. Cf. W.C. Nealo, 'Land Is to Rule', in *Land Control and Social Structure in Indian History* edited by R.E. Frykenberg (New Delhi: Manohar, 1979).

75. Cf. Gazetteer of the Bombay Presidency, vol. IX, part II, *Gujrat Population: Mussalmans and Parsis* (Bombay: Government Central Press, 1899), p. 25.

76. This situation was prevalent also in other parts of India. A curious example can be found among the Komati traders of South India. They were related to the Mādigās (the leather-workers of the 'Telugu country') by an interesting custom. The former had to invite the latter to any marriage ceremony and obtain the Mādigā's consent. If a Mādigā was not satisfied, he could 'effectually put a stop to a marriage by coming to the house at which it was to be celebrated, chopping away

the plantain trunks and carrying them off'. See E. Thurston and K. Rangachari, *Castes and Tribes of Southern India* (Madras: Government Press, 1909), vol. III, p. 327. According to Thurston and Rangachari this custom was a recognition of the lordship exercised by these depressed castes in bygone days.

77. In refutation of this point, it may be said that Banjārās, the leading overland transporters in eighteenth-century India, were armed. However, their failure to observe the code of mutual forbearance prevailing between merchants and landholders or cultivators contributed to their dissolution as a mercantile group. They became marauding bands or nomadic tribes and were hounded by the British as their conquests covered the land.

78. Cf. Ray, *Change in Bengal Agrarian Society*, chapters 2 and 4.

79. For a careful study of the pattern of changes in superior land rights in the Benares region and the reasons for purchase of land by men who had made money as government officials or merchants, see B.S. Cohn, 'Structural Change in Indian Rural Society', esp. pp. 78–9.

80. One symptom of the lack of mobility of property in land or superior revenue-farming rights was that no specialized estate agents or surveyors of the type made familiar by the novels of George Eliot relating to the English countryside ever grew up in colonial India.

Nor could somebody simply decide, following Bingley of Jane Austen's *Pride and Prejudice*, to buy an estate neighbouring that of a friend.

81. Cf. for example, the inventory of assets of Ramdulal De, in P. Sinha, *Calcutta in Urban History* (Calcutta: Firma K.L.M., 1978), pp. 79–80.

82. Cf. Bagchi, 'Reflections on Patterns of Regional growth in India', sections 4 and 5.

83. D.H.A. Kolff, 'A Study of Land Transfers in Mau Tahsil, Jhansi', in Chaudhuri and Dewey (eds.), *Economy and Society*, pp. 61–2.

84. Timberg, *The Marwaris*, chapter 5.

85. G.D. Birla, for example, was described as 'mill-owner, merchant and zamindar', in the *Indian Year-Book 1939–40*. In the same volume, R.K. Dalmia is included in the ranks of 'Indian nobles'.

86. When Awadh *taluqdar*s borrowed from the Bank of Bengal in the 1870s, local *sahukars* were often guarantors of the loans. See my forthcoming *History of the State Bank of India*, vol. I.

87. Gazetteer of the Bombay Presidency, vol. VII, *Baroda* (Bombay: Government Central Press, 1883), p. 392.

88. Gazetteer of the Bombay Presidency, vol. VII, *Baroda*, p. 396.

89. For description of the history of the farming and *potedari* systems, see Gazetteer of the Bombay Presidency, vol. VII, *Baroda*, pp. 392–420.

90. Gazetteer of the Bombay Presidency, vol. VII, *Baroda*, p. 125.

91. For summary accounts of the affairs of William Palmer & Co., see J.W. Kaye, *The Life and Correspondence of Charles, Lord Metcalfe* (London, 1858), vol. II, pp. 31–94; and E. Thompson, *The Life of Charles, Lord Metcalfe* (London: Faber and Faber, 1937), chapter 13.

92. Andhra Pradesh State Archives, Instl. 22, List 2, S. No. 34, file on 'Loans and Advances', 1889. Interesting newspaper reports of loans from *sahukars* are given in Moulvie Syed Mehdi Ali, *Hyderabad Affairs*, vol. II (Hyderabad, 1884).

93. For further information on the firm of Bansilal Abirchand, see Timberg, *The Marwaris*, pp. 136–7.

94. On the origins of the Marwari mercantile communities, see Gadgil, *Origins of the Modern Indian Business Class*, section 6; R.V. Russell and Hira Lal, *The Tribes and Castes of the Central Provinces of India* (first published in 1916; reprinted in Delhi: Cosmo Publications, 1975), vol. II, pp. 116–18. On their position in the Rajput states, see Russell and Hira Lal, *The Tribes and Castes of the Central Provinces of India*, pp. 118–19 and Timberg, *The Marwaris*, chapter 5.

95. The Imperial Gazetteer of India, vol. XIV, *Jaisalmer to Kaira* (Oxford: Clarendon Press, 1908), p. 8.

96. Reprinted in *The English Works of Raja Rammohun Roy*, part I, edited by K. Nag and

D. Burman (Calcutta: Sadharan Brahmo Samaj, 1945).

97. Nag and Burman (eds), *The English Works of Raja Rammohun Roy*, part I, para 12.

98. S.D. Desai, *Mulla's Principles of Hindu Law* (Bombay: N.M. Tripathi, 1978), pp. 85–6.

99. For an account of the organization of indigenous banking in British India, see L.C. Jain, *Indigenous Banking in India* (London: Macmillan, 1929), chapters 2 and 3.

100. The institution of *chaudhuris* is described in detail by Buchanan Hamilton in his report on Bhagalpur. See Montgomery Martin, *The History, Antiquities Topography and Statistics of Eastern India* (1838), vol. II (reprinted in Delhi: Cosmo Publications, 1976), pp. 282–3; and the reasons for the decline of the 'chiefs of trades' are given by F. Buchanan in *An Account of the Districts of Bihar and Patna in 1811–12* (Patna: Bihar and Orissa Research Society, n.d.), vol. II, p. 700.

101. See, in this connection, Bayly, 'Indian Merchants in a Traditional Setting: Benares'.

102. Douglas, *Glimpses of Bombay and Western India*.

103. See Gazetteer of the Bombay Presidency, vol. VIII, *Kathiawar* (Bombay: Government Central Press, 1884), p. 212, and Gazetteer of the Bombay Presidency, vol. IV, p. 74.

104. See the note of the Treasury Officer of Mirzapur enclosed by J.M. Erskine,

officiating Deputy Auditor and Accountant General, United Provinces, in his letter dated 22 December 1862 to the Secretary to the Financial Department, Government, in National Archives of India, Financial Department Proceedings 1864, no. 28. For further details see my forthcoming *History of the State Bank of India*, vol. I.

105. An extract from the report is given in the *Report of the Bombay Chamber of Commerce for the Fourth Quarter 1839–40*, Appendix. This is the house whose further fortunes as the firm of Tarachand Ghanshyamdas have been traced by Timberg in *The Marwaris*, pp. 137–45.

106. Tod, *Annals and Antiquities of Rajasthan*, vol. I, p. 554.

107. See R. Temple, *Men and Events of My Time in India* (London: John Murray, 1882), p. 248, and *Administration Report for Hyderabad for 1869–70*, by C.B. Saunders, British Resident, reprinted in Moulavi Syed Mehdi Ali; *Hyderabad Affairs* (1884), vol. V (Andhra Pradesh Archives), p. 276.

108. W. Crooke, *The Tribes and Castes of the North Western India* (first published, 1896; reprinted in Delhi: Cosmo, 1974), vol. I, p. 164; *Gazetteer of the Rampur State* (Allahabad: Government Press, 1911), p. 15.

109. E. Stokes, 'Rural Revolt in the Great Rebellion of 1857 in India: A Study of the Saharanpur

and Muzaffarnagar Districts', in *Peasants and the Raj* by E. Stokes (Cambridge: Cambridge University Press, 1978).

110. See H.H. Wilson, 'A Sketch of the Religious Sects of the Hindus', *Asiatic Researches*, vol. XVI (first published, 1828; reprinted in Delhi; Cosmo Publications, 1980), pp. 38–42; Jadunath Sarkar, *A History of Dasnami Naga Sanyasis* (Allahabad: Panchayati Akhara Mahanirvani, n.d.), chapter 10; and B.S. Cohn, 'The Role of the Gosaias in the Economy of the Eighteenth and Nineteenth Century Upper India', *IESHR*, I (4), April–June 1964.

111. Gazetteer of the Bombay Presidency, vol. V, *Cutch, Palanpur and Mahi Kantha* (Bombay: Government Central Press, 1880), p. 55. Both in Cutch and in Kathiawar, it was stated that the poorer people among the Lohānas were cultivators, masons, labourers, and vegetable sellers. See Gazetteer of the Bombay Presidency, vol. VIII, *Kathiawar* (Bombay: Government Central Press, 1884), p. 149.

112. Imperial Gazetteer of India, vol. 22 (1908), *Samadhiāla to Singhāna*, pp. 276–7 ('Shikarpur Town') and 407–8 ('Sind').

113. With a general decline of handicrafts and establishment of European control over major arteries of trade and communications, many mercantile communities simply became

agriculturists. For example, *banajigas*, who were a big trading caste of Karnataka at the time Buchanan conducted his survey of the region were reported in 1926 to be mainly agriculturists, 'only a sixteenth part of the caste' being engaged in trade. See Mysore Gazetteer, vol. I, *Descriptive*, edited by C. Hayavadana Rao (Bangalore: Government Press, 1927), p. 213; and also Thurston and Rangachari, *Castes and Tribes of Southern India*, vol. IV, pp. 232–6.

114. See Gazetteer of the Bombay Presidency, vol. IX, part I, *The Gujarat Population: Hindus*, p. 80; Thurston and Rangachari, *Castes and Tribes of Southern India*, vol. III, pp. 308–9.

115. Thurston and Rangachari, *Castes and Tribes of Southern India*, vol. V, p. 252.

116. Gazetteer of the Bombay Presidency, vol. IX, part I, *Gujarat Population: Hindus*, pp. 104–5.

117. Thurston and Rangachari, *Castes and Tribes of Southern India*, vol. III, pp. 309–10.

118. Thurston and Rangachari, *Castes and Tribes of Southern India*, vol. V, p. 253. A very similar account of the sharing of financial responsibility within the family and of the training of the young trader belonging to the *meshri bania* community of Gujarat is given in Gazetteer of the Bombay Presidency, vol. IX, part I, *Gujarat Population: Hindus*, pp. 79–88. Keeping of account books was quite

a sophisticated affair, and demanded a long apprenticeship.

119. Hayavadana Rao, *Indian Review*, 1907, quoted by Thurston and Rangachari, *Castes and Tribes of Southern India*, vol. V, p. 257.

120. Thurston and Rangachari, *Castes and Tribes of Southern India*, vol. V, p. 257 (article on 'Nattukottai Chettis'); and Shoji Ito, 'Business Combines in India—With Special Reference to the Nattukottai Chettiars', *Developing Economics*, 1966.

121. Cf. K.J. Arrow, 'Control in Large Organizations', in *Essays in the Theory of Risk-bearing* by K.J. Arrow (Chicago: Markham, 1971).

122. Gazetteer of the Bombay Presidency, vol. IX, part I, *Gujarat Population: Hindus*, p. 79.

123. Timberg, *The Marwaris*, p. 134.

124. This was the reason for Mohtarim Khan banning the use of *ant* in 1715, for the rise in the value of *ant* had brought all trade virtually to a standstill. See Ali Muhammad Khan, *Mirat-i-Ahmadi*, p. 363.

125. Gazetteer of the Bombay Presidency, vol. IV, *Ahmedabad*, pp. 66–7.

126. Census of India, 1961, vol. V, Gujarat, part VII-B, *Fairs and Festivals* by P.K. Trivedi (Delhi: Manager of Publications, Government of India, 1965), p. 65.

127. Russell and Hira Lal, *Tribes and Castes of the Central Provinces of India*, vol. II, p. 126.

128. Imperial Gazetteer of India, vol. XIII, *Gyaraspur to Jais* (Oxford, 1908), p. 346.

129. Captain T. Macan, deposing before the Select Committee on the Affairs of the East India Company (1831–2) and Colonel Sleeman, writing in 1844, both singled out Indian merchants as being specially interested in the maintenance and stability of British rule. See Macan's evidence in Irish Universities Press reprints of British *Parliamentary Papers*, vol. 6 (1831–2), p. 156; W.H. Sleeman, *Rambles and Recollections of an Indian Official* (London, 1844), vol. II, pp. 142–3.

130. Stokes, *Peasants and the Raj*, pp. 159–74; T.R. Metcalf, *Land, Landlords and the British Raj* (Delhi: Oxford University Press, 1979), chapter 6.

131. A. Joshi, *Lala Shri Ram* (New Delhi: Orient Longman, 1975), pp. 42–3.

132. Budri Dass had amassed so much house property at Ferozepore that the British could not make his son a *kotwal* in succession to him although they wanted to do so. Joshi, *Lala Shri Ram*, p. 41. Among the duties of a *kotwal* at a British cantonment in the 1830s and 1840s was the regulated supply of female campfollowers. See K. Ballhatchet, *Race, Sex and Class under the Raj* (London: Weidenfeld and Nicolaon, 1980), chapter 1.

Index